Center for
Creative Leadership

leadership. learning. life.

About the Center for Creative Leadership

The Center for Creative Leadership is an international, nonprofit, educational institution whose mission is to advance the understanding, practice, and development of leadership for the benefit of society worldwide. Founded in Greensboro, North Carolina, in 1970 by the Smith Richardson Foundation, Inc., the Center is today one of the largest institutions in the world focusing on leadership. In addition to locations in Greensboro; Colorado Springs, Colorado; San Diego, California; and Brussels, Belgium, the Center has an office in New York City and maintains relationships with more than twenty network associates and partners in the United States and abroad.

The Center conducts research, produces publications, and provides a variety of educational programs and products to leaders and organizations in the public, corporate, educational, and nonprofit sectors. Each year through its programs, it reaches more than twenty-seven thousand leaders and several thousand organizations worldwide. It also serves as a clearinghouse for ideas on leadership and creativity and regularly convenes conferences and colloquia by scholars and practitioners.

For more information on the Center for Creative Leadership, call Client Services at (336) 545-2810, send an e-mail to info@leaders.ccl.org, or visit the Center's World Wide Web home page at http://www.ccl.org.

Funding for the Center for Creative Leadership comes primarily from tuition, sales of products and publications, royalties, and fees for service. The Center also seeks grants and donations from corporations, foundations, and individuals in support of its educational mission.

Center for
Creative Leadership
leadership. learning. life.

Valerie I. Sessa
Jodi J. Taylor

Executive
Selection

Strategies for Success

JOSSEY-BASS
A Wiley Company
San Francisco

Center for
Creative Leadership

leadership. learning. life.

Jossey-Bass books and products are available through most bookstores. To contact Jossey-Bass directly, call (888) 378–2537, fax to (800) 605–2665, or visit our website at www.josseybass.com.

Substantial discounts on bulk quantities of Jossey-Bass books are available to corporations, professional associations, and other organizations. For details and discount information, contact the special sales department at Jossey-Bass.

Manufactured in the United States of America on Lyons Falls Turin Book. This paper is acid-free and 100 percent totally chlorine-free.

Library of Congress Cataloging-in-Publication Data
Sessa, Valerie I.
  Executive selection: strategies for success/Valerie I. Sessa, Jodi J. Taylor.
    p. cm.
  "A joint publication of the Jossey-Bass business & management series and the Center for Creative Leadership"—Prelim. p.
  Includes bibliographical references and index.
  ISBN 0–7879–5020–3
  1. Executives—Selection and appointment. I. Taylor, Jodi J. II. Center for Creative Leadership. III. Title. IV. Jossey-Bass business & management series.

HF5549.5.S38 S47 2000
658.4'07112—dc21   00-037091

FIRST EDITION
HB Printing   10 9 8 7 6 5 4 3 2 1

A Joint Publication of

The Jossey-Bass
Business & Management Series

and

The Center for Creative Leadership

*This book is dedicated to
H. Smith Richardson,
whose dreams provided the impetus for this research,
and
Richard J. Campbell,
whose vision turned those dreams into reality.*

Contents

Preface

In the past five years we've seen CEO and top-management failure at such organizations as Apple Computer, Blue Cross–Blue Shield, AT&T, Sunbeam Corporation, and Citicorp. And these failures are devastating to these companies. At AT&T, the severance package for John Walter was $26 million (in addition to his compensation that year of $1 million and an annual pension; Keller, 1998). This figure does not even begin to cover the turmoil, upheaval, and tumult that crippled AT&T's executive suite, the organization, and its stakeholders.

Although it seems that almost everyone can tell a story of a spectacular selection failure, we have found that top executives in many organizations are not approaching the selection of the next generation of leaders with the same zeal or skill with which they approach other challenges related to the state of the organization. Selection decisions are made in an illogical and slipshod manner. Estimates of failure rates start at 27 percent and go as high as 75 percent, and what's most distressing is that these high rates of failure are occurring at the same time that the need for successful top executives is increasing.

The pesky conundrum that many organizations are struggling with is that strong leadership is essential to survival in the current competitive business environment, but the leaders selected to fill important corporate positions are often not doing the job—or the position goes unfilled. In the summer of 1997, there were unfilled CEO and president spots at Unisys, AT&T, Delta Airlines, Quaker

Oats, Apple Computer, Waste Management Corp., and Gateway 2000 (Greco, 1997).

Organizations Need an Effective Method for Selecting Top Leaders

Executives realize that something must be done to improve the selection of the next generation of leaders. They're looking for help, but they're not finding it. They're getting plenty of advice about what they need in their new executives—the competencies, the knowledge, the skills, the abilities, and the characteristics needed to run today's and tomorrow's organization—but virtually nothing about how actually to succeed in hiring the people they need at the very top of their organizations. No one has been able to offer an effective plan. Until now, no one has been able to suggest what must be done to make the selection process effective, how to steer clear of the ranks of those who are failing at selection, how to avoid the major negative consequences that befall organizations when selections fail.

At the Center for Creative Leadership (CCL), we wanted to put selection onto a firmer footing. We wanted to find out how it should be done. We started by asking, "What does it mean to be successful in today's organizations? How can we select executives who are more likely to be successful?"

Our answers came mainly from large-scale research that we have been conducting for the last several years on executive selection. We conducted two major studies, listened to hundreds of executives tell us their tales of selection, both good and bad, and ran a simulation that told us a great deal about the decision-making styles of those who choose top-level executives. In addition, we supplemented our research with our own expertise in dealing with executives at the top and with the management and psychological literature.

This book presents what we have learned from all of these sources. We have synthesized all the information and put it into the form of sequential steps that practicing managers can use to help them understand the important elements that need to be present to make successful top-level selections.

Audience

We wish to assist people who must make selection choices or who are interested in the choices others are making—that is, top-level executives, boards of directors, human resource professionals, search firm professionals, and shareholders—to further their abilities for selecting successful top-level executives. Whether your company is private or public; large, medium, or small; your own firm or one you are interested in; and whether you are in the upper echelons or aspire to be, this practical book is designed to help you develop a successful selection process. The objective is to take the alchemy out of selection and put the science—and the common sense—back in.

For some readers, this will mean an improvement in selection at the very top of their organizations. For others, it will mean knowing what to look for when a company of interest experiences change at the top. And for still others, it will mean the development of new theories and new testable ideas to aid in selecting successful top executives.

Top executives, boards of directors, human resource professionals, and executive search firms can use the book in conjunction with the selection systems and competencies they have in place or are developing in their organizations. They can use it to ensure that they have created the best decision-making process to make the selection and to ensure that they have taken into account important, yet often missed, steps in the selection process.

Those interested in organizations in general or who follow the stock market will be able to assess and make their own conclusions regarding the executive selection process being conducted within companies of interest. Researchers will read the book primarily as a resource for garnering ideas on additional research to conduct in this area. They can take ideas from this book and test them in new and different ways.

A Team-Based Systematic Executive Selection Process

The book is divided into ten chapters. Chapter One describes the precarious state of executive selection in companies today and how researchers at the Center for Creative Leadership approached the topic—our perspectives, the topics we were interested in, and a description of our two large-scale research studies. Chapter Two describes what really matters at the top. Top-level executives told us that they define successful executives based on bottom-line organizational results achieved under those individuals' tenure and on the relationships they maintain with others, particularly their subordinates. The team-based selection system that is described in Chapters Three through Eight use this definition of success and failure as a starting point.

Chapter Three outlines the importance of deciding who should be involved in the selection process. Chapter Four helps selectors develop a systematic, disciplined, and rich way to look at the organization and its environment, the open position, and the candidate requirements. Using this method helps selectors come to an agreed-upon image of an ideal candidate to use throughout the process. Chapter Five emphasizes the importance of developing a good candidate pool. Chapter Six describes the heart of the selection system: deciding whom to hire. In this chapter, we discuss tools used to gather information on candidates and the importance of using the right information. Finally, selection is not over the moment the newly hired executive accepts the position. Chapter Seven explains why it is necessary to provide integration into the organization and continuous development to ensure the success of the executive. In all, these chapters lay out the basic steps in our selection process.

Chapter Eight describes a paradox: top-level executives are increasingly looking outside their organizations for high-level executives yet are struggling with the fact that external executives are less likely to succeed in their organizations. In this chapter, we compare and make suggestions for improving the selection process for both internal hires and external hires.

Chapter Nine provides an easy-to-use guide that summarizes our findings and the suggestions that are detailed in Chapters Three through Eight. After reading this book, you can use this chapter as a handy reference during selection meetings.

Finally, Chapter Ten explains that executive selection does not occur in a vacuum. To be truly successful, executives must have a firm understanding of all the systems in the organization and how decisions that are made in one arena have consequences in all other areas of the organization. This chapter goes beyond the research we have conducted to date. It outlines our next steps in understanding how executive selection affects the ways the organization practices leadership in terms of production, control, learning, and rewards.

The book also includes two appendixes. In Appendix A, we provide the questionnaire and interview protocol used in our first study. In Appendix B, we describe the multimedia simulation we developed and used in our second study.

Selection at the top of organizations is different from the process that takes place lower in the organization. *Executive Selection*, using lessons drawn from those who are on the executive "hiring line," outlines a team-based systematic process that takes the mystery and art out of executive selection and places in it the rational, yet intuitive, decision-making realm that executives use in solving other organizational challenges.

Acknowledgments

Writing a book is often a collaborative effort, not just between the authors but also through the assistance of many others. We thank the following for their contributions to this book: Jennifer Beck, Bruce Byington, Dawn Cecil, Kim Corson, Jennifer Deal, Carey

Edwards, Bernie Ghiselin, Richard Guzzo, George Hollenbeck, Susan Hyne, Robert Kaiser, Pam Kanuch, Mary Leight, Laurie Merritt, Erin Pottratz and the members of Interactive Papyrus, Cheryl Schustack, Garold Stasser, Lisa Szumigala, Mario Trujillo, Whynne Whyman, various interns, the more than one thousand participants in CCL's Leadership at the Peak program, CCL's Leadership at the Peak training and adjunct staff, and the information center at CCL—Peggy Cartner, Kinsey Gimbel, and Carol Keck.

Special thanks to David Day, Bill Drath, Kevin Liu, Cindy McCauley, Ross Mecham, Patricia O'Connor, and Gary Rhodes for their help in constructing Chapter Ten.

For supporting our efforts we are grateful to the Executive Selection Research Advisory Group, which includes John Campbell, David DeVries, Milton Hakel, Susan Jackson, Louis Mattis, Hassan Minor Jr., Lanty Smith, Melvin Sorcher, and Walter Tornow.

Finally, we are grateful to our editorial team: Marcia Horowitz, Martin Wilcox, and Joanne Ferguson, at CCL; Cedric Crocker and Byron Schneider, at Jossey-Bass Publishers in San Francisco; and Allen Venable, developmental editor for Jossey-Bass.

April 2000   Valerie I. Sessa
                                       Greensboro, North Carolina

                                              Jodi J. Taylor
                                       Colorado Springs, Colorado

The Authors

Valerie I. Sessa has been at the Center for Creative Leadership (CCL) for seven years and is a research scientist and a director of New Frontiers, a division designed to bring new thinking and innovation to CCL. Sessa has been codeveloper and manager of a large-scale program of research in the area of executive selection, which included an interview study of high-ranking executives on current selection practices at the very top of organizations. Results of this study were published in the CCL technical report, *Executive Selection: A Research Report on What Works and What Doesn't* (1998).

Sessa also was codesigner and developer of the Peak Selection Simulation, a multimedia simulation designed to study and educate top-level leaders on how to select executives. Some of the results of this study were published in the technical report, *Choosing Executives: A Research Report on the Peak Selection Stimulation* (1999). She has written two other CCL reports on the topic of executive selection: *Selection at the Top: An Annotated Bibliography* (1997) and *Selecting International Executives: A Suggested Framework and Annotated Bibliography* (1999), which begins to address selection in the global arena.

Sessa has made many presentations on executive selection and has written a chapter on the topic for *How People Evaluate Others in Organizations: Person Perception and Interpersonal Judgment in I/O Psychology*, edited by Manuel London (forthcoming).

Sessa is a member of the American Psychological Association, the Academy of Management, North Carolina Industrial and Organizational Psychologists, and the Society for Industrial and Organizational Psychology. She is a graduate of the industrial and organizational psychology doctoral program at New York University (NYU). Before working at CCL, she consulted for a number of large organizations and was an adjunct instructor at NYU, Yeshiva University, and Marymount Manhattan College.

Jodi J. Taylor is president of Summit Leadership Solutions (SLS), a consulting and training firm that helps organizations improve their effectiveness by leveraging their leadership talent to accomplish strategic objectives. SLS provides consulting and training in the areas of assessment, executive selection, executive decision making, leadership development, executive team development, and executive coaching. SLS emphasizes helping organizations become more disciplined and focused in their selection and development of leadership talent. Taylor's clients at SLS have included General Motors, Bell South Enterprises, US West DEX, Maytag Corporation, MediaOne, Atlantic Mutual, Vail Resorts, Starvest Partners, and IgnitionState.com.

Previously, as vice president of CCL, Taylor was responsible for line and staff operations. Both the San Diego and Colorado Springs campuses reported to her, as did all marketing, business development, and customer service divisions. She helped found the Colorado Springs campus and served as its first director from 1987 to 1996. She is codesigner of the Leadership at the Peak program for senior executives and has worked extensively designing development programs to meet the leadership needs of specific organizations. She was the originator and codesigner of Peak Selection Simulation and part of the CCL Executive Selection research team with Valerie Sessa. She served as a member of CCL's executive team, working on strategy, planning, and operational decision making for the entire organization. At CCL, she worked with such companies as General Motors, Prudential, FMC, Maytag, Reader's Digest, Tenneco, Coach, and Ciba-Geigy to help these companies develop their leadership capabilities.

Taylor obtained her Ph.D. in counseling psychology from the University of Texas at Austin. Currently she is on the advisory boards of Colorado Springs Trails, Open Space Parks, and the U.S. Foundation; is a founding member of the Colorado Springs Leadership Institute; and is a member of the board of the Center for Effective Development and Population Activities, an international organization working with women in third-world countries on health issues and leadership development. She speaks to corporate and professional audiences internationally on executive leadership, corporate change, and executive selection.

Executive Selection

Chapter One

The Current State of Executive Selection

Crisis at the Top

> I consider this selection decision one of the single
> most devastating failures of my career.
> *Anonymous executive, 1999*

No single decision affects the survival of an organization more than that of the people selected to run it. Choosing a chief executive or other key top-level personnel is the most important strategic decision that can be made in a business. And the importance of this choice is growing as many CEOs and other top-level executives in today's companies reach retirement age. In 1996 alone, the search for qualified CEOs rose by 28 percent (Greco, 1997).

Top executives were asked to identify the single most lethal weapon executives could employ against a competitor (Ulrich & Lake, 1990). After examining such areas as improving their own product quality and service, taking away a competitor's customers, and reducing a competitor's access to capital, the executives nearly always concluded that the single most important weapon would be to control hiring for six months at a competitor's firm. If they could control who was hired, they could ensure that the competitor would be at a disadvantage not only for six months but over the long term.

Yet, oddly, sometimes it seems as though top executives do not apply this same thinking to themselves. In charge of their own top-level hiring, they often seem little inclined to give it top priority or to practice effective selection techniques for ensuring their company's future. A *New York Times* article reported that executives themselves will tell you that employees are the sine qua non of organizational survival, yet when given the chance to rank the strategies most likely to bring success, they put succession, selection, and other people issues near the bottom (Noble, 1995).

Why? It is easy to push these kinds of issues to the side when there seem to be more burning issues to address. And yet, top management teams are belatedly recognizing that their job is to nourish the organization and the people in it, leaving it better able to perform and survive in the competitive business world. In fact, in our view, too many CEOs are waking up late in their careers when they are close to retirement and suddenly asking, "Where is my next group of leaders going to come from when I have brought no one along with me?"

In one poignant interview, a retired CEO reflected with us on his own very successful and distinguished career. He kept coming back to one critical mistake that he had made in selecting his successor. He said, "I am saddened because the right guy was there but I didn't appoint him. The way I chose my successor was an exercise in how not to do something." Even many years after his retirement, people in the company kept calling him and telling him how much they missed him. He didn't take this as a compliment because he knew that if he had chosen the best person to lead the company into the future they wouldn't still be missing him but would instead be thriving under their new leadership. He told us:

> I didn't approach the decision in a disciplined and methodical way. I didn't seek advice and I didn't think deeply enough. That was so unlike me. I had a reputation for being very disciplined in my decision making, but in this, the most important decision of my career—that of who should succeed me—I chose to ignore data that I had. There had been some real instances where this person had not used good judgment; not a lot, but enough that I should have been more careful. He had all the skills needed to do the job, but

sometimes he wasn't as straightforward as he needed to be and didn't take others' feelings into consideration. He was basically lacking in humanity. Now he leads the company with that lack of humanity. Had I been really disciplined in my decision-making process, I would have seen that in advance. After I left, the company lost an account that they had been taking care of for over one hundred years because of his judgment errors in handling that account. The company will never recover from that loss.

The Precarious State of Executive Selection

Today, the state of selection at the top three levels of the organization is not good. There are a host of reasons why decision makers are either unable or unwilling to address their most important job of selecting the next generation of leaders.

First, executives usually have very little expertise in selection. According to a study by the Center for Effective Organizations (Lawler & Finegold, 1997), top-level executives who sit on typical boards of U.S. corporations lack the skills and knowledge to make effective selection decisions. Boards need to become more effective in skills of selection to avoid serious mistakes—in particular to be able to choose executives based on the company's strategic needs. The authors said: "To use the parlance of mariners, they have been like an oceangoing vessel without an experienced captain who knows both the capabilities and limitations of his crew and his ship. And, as always in the corporate world, there is the certainty that a storm looms ahead" (p. 92).

Second, we have learned from our research that selection is not something executives feel particularly good at. Therefore, they naturally gravitate to what seems to be more pressing (and more manageable): day-to-day issues. In addition, some of the very characteristics that allow executives to succeed may make it difficult for them to face their own mortality. In his book *Beyond Ambition: How Driven Managers Can Lead Better and Live Better*, Robert Kaplan (1991) talks about the expansive personality characteristics of most executives. They thrive on challenge, they strive to master, and their energy and drive fill the empty spaces. They don't want to face their own mortality and so put off unconsciously the need to address succession. It is something they will get to in the future. Some people we interviewed even postulated a darker motivation: that executives need to be seen as indispensable and therefore are unwilling to let go. As a result, they avoid selection issues, or even worse, unconsciously select someone unsuited for the job, setting their successor up for failure. In one company we worked with, the previous CEO and executive team were brought back in to run the company five years after they had all retired because their chosen successors had mismanaged the company so badly.

Third, in making selections executives do not employ the decision-making processes that they use in other decisions. In 1985, Peter Drucker said, "By and large, executives make poor promotion and staffing decisions. By all accounts, their batting average is no better than .333. At most one-third of such decisions turn out right; one-third are minimally effective; and one-third are outright failures. In no other area of management would we put up with such miserable performance." And thirteen years later, Nadler and Nadler (1998) said, "In their most introspective moments, most executives readily acknowledge that selecting the right people for the right jobs constitutes one of their most important responsibilities. Few decisions they make will have as direct an impact on every facet of the organization. Yet, few other decisions are made in such an illogical, slipshod manner" (p. 229). In an example of what they were talking about, a *Fortune* article (Grant, 1997) reports the following:

> When PepsiCo CEO Roger Enrico disclosed his plan to spin off his restaurant division—KFC, Taco Bell, and Pizza Hut—observers asked why he'd jettison a huge enterprise ($10 billion in sales, estimated), before finding the people to run it. The answer is that Enrico had no clear idea at the time who should head up the name-

less new company. Shortly after the announcement, he asked two top contenders to decide who should be No. 1 and No. 2. Unsurprisingly, the two deadlocked, so Enrico took the extraordinary step of hiring a headhunter to find a suitable outsider, at which point Enrico would decide among all three. A PepsiCo spokesman calls this convoluted bake-off "the normal process you'd expect when selecting the leadership of a $10 billion corporation."

Fourth, there are several structural reasons for the current poor situation surrounding the selection of effective executives. In large measure, organizations are not prepared to replace the senior executives who leave with competent replacements from their internal ranks—primarily because they are faced with a short supply of middle managers as a result of downsizing. In addition, many organizations have inadequate hiring, promotional, and succession-planning systems. Given these two factors, companies increasingly look to the outside for their top leaders, where they find that it takes up to five hundred contacts to find the "right" executive for each CEO position ("Top Gunning," 1997) with the often dismaying result that they are not "right" after all.

Fifth, the environment has changed dramatically. Organizations are changing. Leadership demands are changing. The world is becoming more complex, and our progress in the art and science of selection has not kept pace with these demands. The old clichés about having "the right stuff" or "the cream" rising to the top, and the Darwinian concept that the "fittest will survive" are no longer adequate guidelines for choosing successful executives. Further, the consequences of poor choices are greater. With more competitors in a global and diverse marketplace, strategic errors are more likely to have serious consequences.

As mentioned, downsizing and flatter organizational structures have weakened the bench strength of available executives. Those who do make it to the top are compelled to be exceptional leaders because there are no longer enough middle managers to buffer the impact of an unsuccessful top-level executive. And there's a relatively new skill that top executives who manage the complex and diverse internal and external environments need to possess: the ability to work well with other top management executives in their organizations. This is because, increasingly, CEOs are turning to top management teams for help in running these new organizations. Thus, it is imperative that top executives not only be capable of doing their job but also be team players.

Center for Creative Leadership's Decision to Study the Problem

Executives know that failure rates are high and selections are poor, but they don't know why. Thus practitioners have begun to turn to organizational researchers for help. As researchers and practitioners working with issues around executive selection (and involved with selecting executives in our own organization), we were motivated by the abundance of stories of problem CEO and top-management successions that we found in the press, the literature, and the hallway chat of many organizations.

CCL's interest in executive selection formally began through a conference on executive selection held at CCL in 1992 in which experts and others interested in the field shared their knowledge and ideas. That interchange resulted in Dr. Richard J. Campbell and the authors of this book initiating a new program of research in 1993. The research focuses on selection at the top three levels of organizations—CEO and two levels down—with its overall objective being to improve the quality of leadership in organizations by becoming a major generator of applied knowledge about executive selection. The result of that effort is a new conception of how top executive selection should be organized—a system that this book will describe.

The following two sections describe the two areas of knowledge that helped guide our program of research.

Six Perspectives on Selection

First, we realized that the selection process can be seen from a number of different perspectives, each of which must be taken into account for a successful selection. These perspectives are *the analytic or psychometric, the decision making, the negotiation, the political, the socioemotional,* and *the developmental.*

Analytic-Psychometric

This is the most common way in which selection is seen, both by those engaged in the selection of executives and by those who study the selection of executives. This perspective focuses on the job candidates. The emphasis is on the assessment of candidates—using the right tools and assessing the right competencies. Many organizations have processes in place addressing this arena of executive selection already. But these processes by themselves are not enough.

Decision Making

Another way to look at executive selection is to look at the decision makers themselves. The people who make the decision and the way they make it is crucial to selection. What processes do they engage in and why? How do individuals make decisions and how do groups make decisions? What works and what does not? This is the main focus of this book, although you will find the other perspectives as well.

Negotiation

Another way to conceptualize executive selection is as the beginning of a relationship between the organization and the potential candidates. Executive selection is a series of negotiations occurring within the organization and between the organization and the candidates. Negotiation occurs in two arenas. First, constructive negotiation can occur in the group of people making the selection. One of the executives we interviewed told us, "An organizational factor that contributed to the selection and to the eventual success of the selected person was that about four different people profited from this selection due to a domino effect that freed up several other spots and a company reorganization." Second, negotiation occurs between the people in the organization making the selection decision and the potential candidates for the position.

Political

Another perspective that must be kept in mind is the political one. Viewed from this angle, selection does not necessarily mean putting the best person into the position. One executive told us about an executive his top-management team had selected and who failed, "Everyone on the selection team wanted another candidate. This person was selected even though he was expected to fail because he was expected to retire in a few years and the company would rather that happen than that he leave early and take his contacts with him."

This perspective takes into account the larger arena in which the decision is being made. For example, if one executive is selected over another, what message does that send to the organization? And what is the impact on the candidates not chosen?

Socioemotional

Often past experiences—positive or negative—influence how selectors unconsciously make decisions. The socioemotional perspective involves the emotional component of decision making about people. It also acknowledges that there are other criteria by which people are judged—namely, the feelings those people evoke in the decision makers. The importance of this perspective is suggested by a statement from one of the executives we interviewed: "The committee only established adequate criteria after being burned by the reaction of the corporate office to their initial desire to choose someone whom they all liked."

Developmental

Like the political perspective, the developmental perspective acknowledges that selection is often not a procedure to put the best person into a position. Instead, the goal in this case is to develop executives to be prepared for future positions. This perspective acknowledges that selection and development are highly interrelated processes. We use this perspective in Chapter Eight when we consider differences between selections of internal executives and selections of external executives.

Our Topics of Investigation

In addition to taking the six perspectives into account in preparing to do our research, we also developed a set of topics to help us frame our research questions. These topics included *organizational needs, position requirements, candidate requirements, candidate pools, match of candidates with requirements, management of the executive, executive performance,* and *organizational results.* We briefly define and discuss each of these content areas in the following paragraphs.

Organizational Needs

The right person hired can help drive the strategy, help fulfill a major organizational gap, and provide the needed leadership skills. But the big question even before we get to the person is how we define what constitutes "right." What is going on in and around the organization as a whole? That is what drives the executive selection process—whether these factors are consciously taken into account or not. They include culture, values, vision, strategy, management approach, goals, structuring, degree of globalization, bottom line, competition, organizational life cycle, and new laws and new policies, to name a few.

It is also important to understand if and how top executives define and assess the organization's environment—both inside and outside—when preparing to select an executive for an open position. We believe that being clear about organizational needs is critical. Understanding its own culture allows the organization to express core values, goals, and beliefs and then to restate them as needed candidate traits and abilities. As a result, candidates' knowledge, skills, abilities, and characteristics can be systematically compared with what the organization needs (Sessa, Kaiser, Taylor, & Campbell, 1998).

Position Requirements

The second topic in executive selection is how top-level executives define success on the job. This definition includes the purpose of the job, its position in the company and how this job links to other roles, the responsibilities, and the relationships it entails, including those with the boss, subordinates, peers, and team members. These requirements are used to define how success will be measured.

Candidate Requirements

The third topic is how top executives deduce from both the position requirements and the organizational needs what they should look for in potential candidates. We divided the candidate requirements into two types*: *hard-side requirements* are concrete and measurable abilities, such as what the individual must know to accomplish the job (his or her behaviors, knowledge, and skills)

---

*Note: Types are based on the writings of Barnard (1938/1950), Borman and Motowildo (1993), and Katz and Kahn (1978).

and what resources the executive must have to be competent (such as relevant job experiences, educational levels, and specific degrees); *soft-side requirements* are those that are more abstract or are inferred, such as abilities and personal characteristics and styles.

We wanted to understand better how top-level executives transform organizational needs and position requirements from context and content statements into behaviors, knowledge, skills, abilities, personal characteristics, experiences, and other attributes that can be assessed both during the selection process and once the executive is onboard.

We believe that the hard-side and soft-side requirements need to be developed from both the position requirements and the organizational needs; an executive's "fit" with the organization is as critical as his or her proficiency and knowledge base.

Candidate Pools

Another topic we wanted to understand better is how top executives create a pool of qualified and attractive candidates. Organizations recruit executives and other employees (either internally or externally) to add to, maintain, or readjust their workforce. The rationale for having a candidate pool (that is, more than one candidate) is that the "best" executive may be chosen for (and choose to accept) the position. The candidate pool needs to identify not only executives with the ability to perform in the position but also executives who will accept an offer.

Who is currently being recruited at the top executive levels? A recent review of the executive selection literature suggests that candidate pools are predominantly middle-aged, middle-class white men with traditional backgrounds. These candidates are motivated to move up the ranks of the organization although they do not necessarily demonstrate good leadership capabilities. In addition, these candidates are increasingly being brought in from the outside as opposed to promoted or selected from within (Sessa & Campbell, 1997).

Match of Candidates with Requirements

Matching the candidates with the requirements is the heart of the selection process. How do decision makers assess what available candidates can bring to the organization and match them to the organizational, job, and candidate requirements? We were also interested in how the candidates assess the organization and its requirements and match these to their own wants, needs, and goals. This portion of the selection process involves a series of trade-offs. No one candidate exactly fits the needs of the organization. What is critical? What can we do without, develop, or change? What if the executive we deem to be the best candidate does not want the position?

We discovered that studying the organization's matching process raises two separate questions. The first is, who is chosen to make the actual selection decision? The second is, what processes are used to make the selection?

In the overall decision process, the matching process—that is, assessing the fit between the candidates and the company's needs and requirements—is what many people think of or want to accomplish when they hear the words *executive selection*. Doing so involves getting relevant information on candidates and using it to assess the match between what the organization and the job need and what each candidate has to offer.

Management of the Executive

A topic that we found was related to and important to consider along with selection is that of managing the transition of a new executive into the position. We divided this topic into two parts.

One concern involves the beginning or socialization process. Because it can take an executive up to two and a half years to master the position (Gabarro, 1987), the success of a selection process cannot be gauged when the final decision is made and the offer accepted. How the executive is introduced to the organization and how the organization is introduced to the executive are part of the process. The socialization phase includes expectations and anticipations before the first day in the position, the actual transition into the position, and adjustment and stabilization for both executives and their organizations (Nicholson & West, 1989).

The second concern with managing the executive has to do with executive development and succession planning. These subjects are covered extensively in a multitude of other materials, including training programs and corporate universities, assessment instruments, computer programs, and books and articles. It is not our intention to add to this body of knowledge but rather to demonstrate that executive selection and executive development intersect at this point. Selection implies development, and development implies selection.

Executive Performance

Another topic we wanted to understand is executive performance. Performance is what the organization hires an executive to do. It is not the consequence or results of the action but the action itself—that which is wholly under the control of the individual executive.

Measuring performance is a critical component of selection. It encompasses everything that ultimately defines success on the job. Performance should be directly related to whether the executive is providing the attributes listed in the organizational needs, the job requirements, and the candidate requirements.

As an executive moves up in the organization, job scope (breadth, number of units), scale (internal complexity, diversity, and ambiguity), and accountability broaden considerably, especially for the CEO job. Because of this complexity, measurements for success in higher levels of the organization are increasingly difficult to define. For example, although CEO success is often measured by a host of financial ratios and stock price as well as the "satisfaction" of the board of directors, Wall Street, stakeholders, and the media, should we hold the CEO or top-management team accountable for the entire organization? What kind of time frame is appropriate? And should we consider how "well" they lead, along with what they achieve in organizational results?

Measuring performance is important to the selection process. As one executive told us, "You hire the résumé but unfortunately the whole person shows up." Once the executive is on the job it becomes clear that the person is more complex than the attributes for which he or she was selected. Success is the result of an emergent dynamic process between executives, the people they work with, and the organization.

In view of this reality, measuring performance is important for three different constituents. For the selectors, it provides feedback about how well their selection process proceeded and provides them with ideas about what they did really well and should repeat during the next selection and what they did poorly and should not repeat. For executives, it provides feedback on how the organization is viewing their performance. If they are told that they are perceived positively, they will continue working in the same manner. If they are told that there is something they need to do differently, then that gives them a chance to try an alternative way of proceeding. For the organization as a whole, it provides feedback on where development needs to take place and where strengths and weaknesses lie in the organization.

Organizational Results

The final topic we explored is organizational results. Organizational results are the goods or services that the organization produces that are exchanged for value. Because organizational results are affected by circumstances beyond its control, they are distinct from and more than the sum of the job performance of all the individuals in an organization.

Understanding results is important to the selection process. Organizational results can be measured as the ratio of outcomes to the cost of achieving the outcomes. Research demonstrates that

CEOs, other high-level executives, and top executive teams have an impact on the bottom line of an organization, including organizational results, reputation, and mortality as well as innovations and strategic change (see Sessa & Campbell, 1997).

Our Research

With the different perspectives in mind and our topic areas targeted, we designed two large-scale research studies—each very different from the other—so that we could verify our findings in two different ways. In both projects we wanted to learn several things: How does selection take place in today's organizations? What drives companies to look inside or outside for executives? How are executives defined as successful and unsuccessful? And what leads to a successful selection? We turned to high-level executives to find the answers.

In our first effort, begun in the fall of 1993, we asked almost five hundred executives in the top three levels of organizations (again, CEO and two levels down) to tell us about a selection in which they had personally participated in the past few years. With about half of the executives, we asked them to discuss a selection that turned out to be successful. With the remainder, we asked them to talk about one that ultimately ended in failure. We also asked the executives why this selection was labeled a success or a failure. We asked them very detailed questions about the selection processes used for that particular selection. And we asked them some general questions about selection in their companies overall.

From these interviews we gained very detailed information about how selection *really* takes place in organizations—not how corporate materials *say* selection should happen, not what appears in the public press, but authentic stories of how selection really happens.

Our nearly five hundred informants were participants in the Leadership at the Peak (LAP) training program offered at the Center for Creative Leadership's Colorado Springs campus. Most of them were white (94 percent), male (90 percent), with an average age of forty-six (ranging from twenty-eight to sixty-three). Some 34 percent were CEOs, 59 percent were in the second level, and 6 to 7 percent were in the third level down.

Participants were predominantly in for-profit organizations (83 percent). They came from such Fortune 500 companies as Allied Signal, AT&T, Avery Dennison, Avon, Bausch & Lomb, Chase Manhattan, Chubb, Coca-Cola, Corning, Dell Computer, Eastman Kodak, GM, Hilton Hotels, Knight Ridder, Kroger, Motorola, The New York Times, Pacificare, PepsiCo, Prudential, Pitney Bowes, Sara Lee, Schering-Plough, Time Warner, TRW, Wells Fargo, and Xerox. Some came from large nonprofits such as the American Heart Association and United Way, some from large government institutions such as the United States Army and the United States Air Force.

Executives were drawn from companies of all sizes: 30 percent were from companies employing 50,000 or more; 28 percent from companies of 10,000 to 49,000; 29 percent from companies of 1,000 to 9,999; and 13 percent from companies of fewer than 1,000 employees. For a look at the questionnaire and interview protocols, see Appendix A. For a detailed look at this study, see our technical report *Executive Selection: A Research Report on What Works and What Doesn't* (Sessa, Kaiser, Taylor, & Campbell, 1998).

In our second effort, begun in the fall of 1995, we observed top executives and top-executive groups that were actually participating in a simulation of the selection of an executive for a top-level position. This simulation was conducted as a part of LAP. The demographics of these top-level executives paralleled those of the first study.

In the course of observing hundreds of participants, we determined what kinds of information executives pay attention to when they assess candidates. The information from over one hundred teams allowed us to assess the typical decision-making processes teams use when making a selection decision, what information they find to be important, and how executives negotiate their decisions within those teams. We were able to draw conclusions about what works and what doesn't, what executives know they should be doing and aren't doing during the selection process, and what executives do that they shouldn't. For a description of the simulation, see Appendix B.

What We Learned

What we learned is the topic of this book. The results of our research efforts are striking: both in their refutation of some current selection wisdom and in their support of other selection practices. In a few words, the best executive selection is practiced as a team-based, disciplined, and systematic process. The process starts with understanding what it means to be successful at the top of an organization. It includes deciding who should be part of the selection decision, developing candidate requirements from organizational needs and position requirements, creating a pool of highly qualified candidates, making the final decision, and helping the executive transition into the position. Chapters Two through Eight spell out what to do to ensure a successful selection process.

Although the current state of selection in American companies is weak, it is hopeful that many executives know that they need to improve in this area. The executives who participated in our research took a serious interest in what we were doing. For these reasons, we believe that this book will be of great assistance.

Chapter Two

Success and How to Get There

What really matters at the top? What actually differentiates successful executives from unsuccessful executives? In this chapter we outline how top-level executives are judged as successful or unsuccessful in their positions. If there is no understanding of what it means to succeed or fail at the top, it is impossible to design or improve an organization's executive selection process. To determine what really matters, we compared the testimony of selectors who had hired a successful candidate with those who had hired an unsuccessful candidate. This chapter reveals a few surprising discrepancies between the ways in which new hires are often evaluated and what ultimately defines their success. At the end of this chapter, we briefly summarize the team-based selection system that the next chapters describe in detail, a system that we developed based on the definitions of success and failure outlined in this chapter.

What Is Success?

In our interviews, the first question we asked was, "Why was this executive considered successful or unsuccessful?" We asked for specifics. The executives in our interview study described the dimensions or categories they used to evaluate the executives they hired. These criteria could be divided into three main categories: *performance*, *relationships*, and *results*.

We discovered that when evaluating executives they have hired, over 75 percent of top-level executives mention using some type of performance indicators, such as pursuing ideas, making forecasts, following through on commitments, demonstrating technical expertise, and demonstrating other job-related skills. As we noted in Chapter One, performance is what the organization hires an executive to do; it is not the consequences or the ultimate result of the action. In addition, 68 percent of our responding executives said that they evaluate top-level executives based on the relationships the executives have with others. They mentioned such things as ability to get along with people and relationships with subordinates. Finally, over half of the executives we interviewed told us that top-level executives are responsible for bottom-line organizational results.

The criteria given by the executives we spoke with are similar to those that executives and organizational experts have used in the past to evaluate executives. In the early 1990s, David DeVries found that executives measure success through performance ratings. To define success, they also look at how fast an executive has been promoted in the organization and how fast his or her compensation has risen. In other words, *indicators of success* are used to define a person as successful. In terms of results or outcomes, executives are evaluated using short-term organizational profitability measures, including a host of financial ratios and stock prices, and the "satisfaction" of the board of directors, Wall Street, and the media. Finally, past CCL research has evaluated the success of executives by determining whether they are engaged in continuous on-the-job learning and development. We have done so on the assumption that executives who continue to learn, develop, and adjust on the job—dealing with poor bosses, their own flaws, and crises and triumphs—are the most successful, whereas those executives who stop learning or adjusting to new situations are more likely to fail.

Three Areas of Evaluation

It seems logical that selectors should evaluate executives on the three categories of performance, relationships, and bottom-line organizational results. The more interesting question is what actually differentiates successful top-level executives from those who are seen as unsuccessful. So we posed another question: What were the executive's critical strengths and weaknesses? In answer, executives gave us specific information regarding the strengths *and* the weaknesses of the particular executive they were recalling.

Surprisingly, we found that performance indicators *did not* differentiate successful from unsuccessful executives. Successful executives need to demonstrate both good organizational results *and* good relationships, particularly with subordinates. But many executives feel there is an inherent tension between a bottom-line orientation and a relationship orientation. A quote from "Chainsaw" Al Dunlap provides an example of this kind of thinking: "If you want a friend, get a dog. I'm not taking any chances. I've got two dogs." Al Dunlap was known for his two-pronged strategy during his tenure at Sunbeam—firing half the workforce and berating the other half, earning him the nickname, "Chainsaw Al." Sunbeam Corporation later fired him when he failed to show results ("Exit Bad Guy," 1998).

Performance

Except in severe cases of misconduct, strengths and weaknesses in performance rarely make the difference between successful and unsuccessful executives.

The most commonly mentioned *strengths* of *unsuccessful* executives were performance strengths. Unsuccessful executives were seen as strong in their technical expertise and other knowledge, skills, abilities, and characteristics needed for their jobs. In fact, they were seen to be as strong in their technical skills as successful executives were. Ironically, however, the most commonly mentioned *weakness* of *successful* executives also fell in the performance category—a lack of particular knowledge, skills, abilities, and characteristics needed for the position.

Why do these typical performance assessments no longer help us differentiate between successful and unsuccessful executives? There are two reasons. The first reason goes back to our original problem of defining what it means to be successful in an executive position. Because there is no one "right way" to perform, two different executives may do the job entirely differently yet both be considered successful. The second reason is that executives who have made it this far up the hierarchy no longer differ enough from each other on performance measures for us to use these measures to distinguish between them.

We are not saying that performance indicators should be discounted entirely. But a different emphasis should be placed on them. Unfortunately, during the selection process and when assessing executives, performance indicators are often the easiest to define, select for, and recognize. The executives making selections seemed to be able to take all these steps fairly well. But they need to be made aware of the fact that performance attributes alone no longer differentiate successful executives from unsuccessful executives. More important are bottom-line organizational results; executives implicitly assess these but do not realize the extent to which they hold executives accountable for them. Relationship skills are also very important to select for, but they are more difficult to articulate, select for, and assess.

The shift from assessing executives' performance to holding them accountable for actual organizational outcomes and their relationships is a big shift in emphasis. Although making this shift implicitly makes sense, it is primarily unspoken and unacknowledged when the shift occurs. It is important that executives understand this shift and determine at what point in the hierarchy of their organization the shift takes place.

Relationships

As already noted, our interviews showed that whether executives are seen as successes or failures depends on their relationships with others, particularly subordinates. The rightness of this view is supported in other recent research. A recent Gallup poll found that good relationships are key to attracting, focusing, and keeping the most talented employees (Buckingham & Coffman, 1999). Relationships are linked to bottom-line organizational performance in terms of productivity and profit (Pfeffer & Viega, 1999). A study published in *Fortune* (Charan & Colvin, 1999) suggests that successful relationships include both nurturing and pruning. For example, the article suggests that General Electric's Jack Welch likes to spot people early, follow them, stretch and grow them, and evaluate them. He tells those who do not have what it takes that GE is not the place for them. The same study suggests that some top-level executives overdo the nurturing and fail to deal with the pruning.

In one company we worked with, we gathered 360-degree assessment data from several hundred executives. In analyzing which characteristics distinguished those executives who scored in the top quartile from those in the bottom quartile, we found that executives who scored in the top quartile showed more openness to and concern about the people they worked with and expected more openness and caring in return. In other words, they behaved in ways that helped create a more open, safe, and concerned environment with their coworkers.

The executives we spoke with did not use the term *emotional intelligence*—a term that is currently gaining popularity in the business press as a necessary element for executive success. However, the ability to maintain high-quality relationships is one important component of this capacity to recognize one's own feelings and those of others, and for managing emotions well in oneself and in one's relationships (Mayer, Caruso, & Salovey, in press). Yet, during the selection process candidates are rarely evaluated on the quality of their relationships, except under the more general heading of interpersonal skills. For example, one executive, speaking of an unsuccessful selection, said, "There is a strong adversarial nature to the job, and the group needed the camaraderie of each other in order to deal with this. The person selected had all the technical skills but was a loner who remained isolated and aloof. He rarely saw the need for normal chitchat and rarely went to lunch with anyone."

To be fair, executives in our study did say that they needed to consider or did consider interpersonal skills at several points during the selection process. Forty percent mentioned that having such skills was a requirement, but only one-fourth of the candidates were specifically assessed on and chosen because of their interpersonal skills. It is also important to note that the interpersonal skills that are accessible in a selection situation are quite different from relationship skills. Although relationship skills and interpersonal skills are similar, relationship skills are much deeper and longer-term, lasting over a long period of time. In contrast, interpersonal skills are broader and can be more superficial.

One senior vice president of a Fortune 100 company told us about a difference between the company's president and the CEO that really explains the difference between relationship skills and interpersonal skills. He mused, "You know, our CEO is a very quiet person and he is not very charismatic, yet I know he really cares about me as a person. Recently, I was in the hospital seriously ill and he was the first person to visit. On the other hand, our president has great interpersonal skills. He is very dynamic and he can talk to anyone. Yet not only did he never visit me in the hospital, but I was back at work for two weeks before he ever even asked me how I was feeling. I don't think he cares about me as a person at all."

Understanding the distinction between interpersonal skills and relationship skills is critical to understanding executive success. Interpersonal skills are needed to survive a cocktail hour, a business meeting, a conference, or a job interview. But relationship skills are needed to sustain working with the same individuals over a long period of time. We do want our executives to be good with people, to be persuasive and skilled in communication and interacting with others, to present the company story, and to be quick on their feet. They need to be credible to the public. And these skills are relatively easy to measure. Yet we may err in assuming that the interpersonal skills that may surface readily in the course of a selection process also signal good relationship skills. Relationship skills must develop over time. They are harder to judge at first glance and during superficial meetings (for example, interviews) with executives. Yet for real work to be done, people need to work in an environment where they feel valued for who they are and where they feel safe to take risks and offer their own opinions. Executives with real relationship skills create environments where people are motivated to do their best. This, of course, directly affects the ability to achieve bottom-line results.

Bottom-Line Organizational Results

Top-level executives are held accountable for the well-being of their organizations. When the organization does well—either based on actual financial ratios or the opinions of outside experts (for example, Wall Street)—the executive is deemed a success. When the organization does poorly, the executive in charge is seen as a failure.

It is difficult to make a direct association between bottom-line organizational results and individuals. Although ratios of financial performance define the goals of the organization, a host of situational and environmental factors affect those outcomes over and above anything for which an individual can and should be held accountable. Such factors as a change in governmental policies or in competitors, an environmental crisis (for example, earthquakes, floods, poisoned goods, or even a war), a workers' strike in a supporting industry, newly elected governmental officials, and the dollar's fluctuating value can all influence the bottom-line result. It is difficult to confidently assess the factors within executives' control and not hold them accountable for the factors that are beyond their control.

Four Conclusions About Success

To summarize what has been said thus far, our findings on the differences between successful and unsuccessful executives suggest four things. First, the success and failure of the organization rests on the shoulders of top-level executives. If the organization does well, the executive is seen to be successful. Conversely, if the organization does poorly, the executive is seen as a failure. This seems logical.

After all, we need to hold someone accountable for the well-being of the organization. However, we must remember that bottom-line results are a combination of many factors, only one of which is one top-level executive.

Second, relationships are equally important, particularly relationships with subordinates. Yet in-depth relationships are rarely considered during the selection process. In addition, although interpersonal skills—a related area—are mentioned as important candidate requirements 40 percent of the time, they are used to assess and choose candidates only one-fourth of the time.

Third, at the top of organizations, performance indicators do not discriminate very well between executives who are successful and those who are not—unless there are severe cases of misconduct (signs indicating an executive is clearly not doing his or her job, such as making sloppy or no forecasts, not meeting goals, not making decisions that need to be made). We believe that performance indicators are the original criteria for entry into the executive ranks. Thus, it is likely that executives who have made it this far will already have them. We do not suggest throwing out performance indicators entirely. Instead, we need to put them in their proper perspective. Although they may be relatively easier to assess, they nevertheless make up only one category of factors to assess.

Finally, we offer a message to the executive who is looking to move into the top ranks. It is worth noting what is *not* mentioned in evaluating the success and failure of the executives. In our research, at no point was the executive's quality of life mentioned. Satisfaction with the position and commitment to the organization played no part in the evaluation of whether they were a success or a failure.

A Team-Based Systematic Selection Process for Getting to Success

We developed the team-based selection system described in this book based on the indicators of success described in this chapter. New hires who demonstrate good bottom-line organizational results and who have good relationships with others, particularly subordinates, are seen as successful. Those who do not demonstrate good bottom-line organizational results and who do not have good relationships are seen as failures.

This section summarizes our team-based systematic selection process research findings. Key aspects of the process are *using a team during the selection process, spending time carefully mapping the challenge, recruiting quality talent, making the decision, integrating the new hire,* and *dealing with the paradigms governing internal and external candidates.*

Use a Decision-Making Team

Our research findings show that teams of top leaders are more likely to select successful executives than are individual top leaders. A variety of executives need to be included on this team (specifically, senior human resource directors, subordinates, and customers), and special consideration must be given to who should be on the team and who should not.

We suggest that choosing a small team that includes a variety of executives to make the selection decision is critical for gaining a range of accurate information, buy-in from the executives involved, and the early development of relationships with the candidates. We also suggest that team dynamics be considered to ensure an open, viable decision-making process.

Map the Challenge

We found that top-level executives who are more explicit in describing the organizational needs, position requirements, and candidate requirements are more likely to hire a candidate who is successful. We also found that it is more difficult to hire successful executives, especially executives from outside the organization, during periods of organizational change, including mergers and acquisitions, and cultural and strategic changes.

It is important to spend time and energy in this stage of the selection process. Being as explicit as possible at this stage ensures that all important information is considered, different perspectives are brought out and heard, there is understanding and a common language for describing what the newly hired executive will do, and everyone involved is in agreement.

Attract Quality Talent

Despite strides made in succession planning, the growing popularity of search firms, and the knowledge that there is a "war for talent" (Chambers, Foulon, Handfield-Jones, Hankin, & Michaels, 1998), the number of qualified candidates considered for top-level positions is small. The typical top executive selected in today's organizations is white, middle-aged, and male. The pool from which the selected candidate is drawn is also predominantly white, middle-aged, and male. We found that including top-quality "nontraditional" individuals in the candidate pool may be beneficial. For example, the presence of a variety of candidates in the pool serves to make the selectors more aware of their selection criteria and their comparison methods.

Make the Decision

Top-level executives rely primarily on interviews, résumés, and references when collecting information about the candidates in the pool. They do not often use the more sophisticated selection tools available such as individual assessments, assessment centers, or tests. However, what seems to be more important than the type of selection tools used is the type of information used to make the selection decision. Selectors who collect and use information that is applicable to their candidate requirements—including information on hard-side skills, soft-side skills, and fit to the position and organization—are more likely to choose a successful candidate. We suggest that using tools appropriate for gathering the required information, gathering good information, and using a decision process that encompasses both rational methods and intuition will lead to selecting the most appropriate candidate.

Integrate the New Executive

Less than one-third of newly hired executives receive any sort of integration or development after assuming their new position. Less than one-quarter receive support from their superiors, and very few receive support from other executives, including peers, subordinates, and customers. However, those who do receive integration and support are more likely to be successful than those who do not. We suggest that both the new hire and the organization need to be prepared. The new hire needs to learn the ropes, learn the culture, learn the politics and power dynamics, and master the transition into the new position. The organization needs to be prepared for the new hire—much as a body needs to be prepared for an organ transplant. This is especially true if the new hire is expected to be an agent of change.

Deal with the Paradigms Governing Internal and External Candidate Hires

Increasingly, companies select top-level executives from outside the organization. We found, however, that once on the job, external hires are less likely to be successful than internal hires. Why is this so?

First, external executives are more likely to be brought in when the organization is undergoing change. They are chosen because they have something that the top-level executives believe the organization needs. Internal executives are promoted because they are seen to have potential and this particular position will help develop them.

Second, selectors use different tools to get different information on external and internal candidates in the candidate pool. We speculate that external executives appear more positive than internal executives because the information gathered on them is both more limited and more weighted toward the positive. In contrast, it is easier to get balanced information on internal candidates that includes both strengths and weaknesses.

Third, because of the preceding two factors, organizations have different expectations for external executives than for internal executives. External executives are seen from a *selection paradigm:* they are chosen for the specific qualities that the organization perceives it needs, with little thought given to the fact that they may need to be developed in some areas. They are expected to perform immediately but not given the support to do so. When they are unable to perform, they are fired. Internal executives are seen from a *developmental paradigm:* they are chosen because they have demonstrated that they have potential, even though there is a clearer picture of their strengths and weaknesses. They are not expected to be perfect. We suggest that it would be useful to combine the selection and development paradigms in the selection process of all candidates.

Summary

We found that proceeding through each of the steps in this team-based systematic selection process leads to the selection of more successful top-level executives. We suggest that selection committees use all of them. Some of them may fit easily into your own company's typical selection process. Some may mesh with other steps that you have found work in your specific situation. And some may require a substantial change in your current selection process. Beginning with a chapter on designing your selection committee, the next six chapters discuss in detail our team-based systematic selection process.

Chapter Three

Deciding Who Should Be Involved

The most powerful hidden dynamic in selection is the decision-making process of the selection committee. As a result, deciding who to involve and how to involve them is a crucial step in the selection process. Carefully choosing the committee is critical to making the right choice among the actual candidates. We saw numerous examples of decision making derailed by hidden agendas of committee members in ineffective group processes. However, this critical step is often completely ignored, and when attended to, often done in a random and haphazard manner.

Why the Selectors Are Important

The person or persons involved in making the selection bring their own perspectives to the decision; they interject something of themselves—their beliefs, biases, past experience, and projections—into the process.

The selectors at the top are different from selectors at the lower levels of the organization. At the lower levels, decisions are often guided with the help of the human resource department. These people know what selection tools are available and how to use them. In contrast, at the upper levels the process is usually undertaken by senior executives, the CEO, and others who may know little about the formal aspects of selection and may have engaged in only a limited number of selections at this level. On the one hand, executives are accustomed to making decisions across a whole variety of complex situations—and doing it well. On the other hand, they are often unaware of their own personal blind spots, and the power of their position may prevent them from getting feedback about and insight into these weaknesses.

Selecting the selectors is important. Individuals who have different relationships to the open position can offer different perspectives. For example, an employee in a subordinate position has a different view of the position than the CEO; in turn, the CEO has a different view than a customer. A greater number of perspectives among the selectors creates a richer view of potential candidates.

Who Currently Makes Top-Level Selection Decisions?

A variety of executives do have a say in the decision-making process. In our research, we found that the executives most likely to be involved are the CEO (or owner of the business), the new hire's superior, and others above the new hire. In contrast, it is rare that the people who are most affected by the decision—subordinates and customers—are involved. An important source of information, the person for whom a replacement is being sought, is largely ignored in the selection process (such individuals are involved 7 percent of the time) even though that person may have the best overall knowledge of the position and its subtleties. Peers are mentioned one-third of the time. Human resource departments are used in one-third of the selections; apparently their specialized knowledge and expertise in selection are not, to a great extent, being taken into account. If we consider also the fact that the executives involved do not appear to have much experience in selecting at the top three levels of the organization (20 percent of the executives we spoke to originally couldn't participate in our study because they had never participated in a selection at the top three levels of the organization!), this suggests to us that they would do well to consider seeking expert advice in this particular task. (See Table 3.1.)

What needs to be taken into account to ensure a top-notch selection committee?

Table 3.1 Executives Involved in High-Level Executive Selections.

Who Is Involved	Percentage of Executives Mentioning
Boss of position	67
CEO, president, or owner of company	66
Human resource department	36
Peers of the boss	33
Peers of the position	31
Chairman of the board	20
Boss's boss	20

Note: N = 322
Source: Sessa, Kaiser, Taylor, & Campbell, 1998.

Use a Team

Although teams at the top are not necessarily the solution in every situation, our research indicates that they dramatically improve the success rate in the selection process. We found that selection decisions are made in one of three ways: an individual makes the selection alone, an individual makes the decision but consults with others, or a team makes the selection together.

The way that the decision is reached—individually, in consultation, or by team consensus—partly determines whether the candidate is successful or unsuccessful. Both our studies found that success improved dramatically when the decision maker consulted with others or when a team made the decision. A team of decision makers allows for greater *range and accuracy of information, buy-in,* and acknowledgment of *the importance of relationships in the executive position.*

Range and Accuracy of Information

During decision making, when executives find that critical information is missing, they generate default information to put in its place based on the way they believe things "ought to be" (Melone,

1994).This is a normal part of any decision-making process and most executives—most people, in fact—are scarcely aware that they do it. However, because different executives have different perspectives, a team discussion allows for greater accuracy and clarity. It also allows executives to challenge each other's unconscious assumptions. Using a team to make the decision can build more rigor into the process. For example, Jon Nicholas, vice president of human resources at Maytag, is very intentional about the people he involves in selection. He told us, "I look for people whose judgment I value and people who will come at the selection from a different viewpoint. I know people on the committee well enough to know how to interpret their information. Sometimes, even if the person has an agenda, they pick up on something that is useful for the committee to consider."

However, it is critical to ensure that there is an effective team process. Decision makers must be candid with each other, able to set aside their own political agendas, handle conflict in a mature fashion, and listen to shared information before making the decision. An effective team process enables members to bring out and use more information in decision making than a single executive can do alone.

The process is not always effective. For example, one committee in our simulation had actually done a great job analyzing the needs of the organization, had clearly stated the skills necessary to create the success, and had prioritized the candidate requirements. The committee members had developed a good process for analyzing the appropriate information. Unfortunately, one member had a know-it-all attitude, was a poor listener, and was very competitive with the other committee members. He was adamantly in favor of one candidate who in fact turned out to be the best candidate by the process the committee had designed. The committee, however, was so annoyed by this particular member's behavior that his advocacy of the candidate became a stumbling block. No way was the committee going to let this annoying member be right! As a result, when it became clear that "his candidate" was the number one choice, they scratched their entire decision-making system and started over. Most amazing, during the postdecision discussion it became clear that the committee members were not aware that they had even engaged in this ineffective process!

Numerous times we have also seen selection decisions skewed by political considerations or by certain members' advocating a choice that does not threaten their own positions. For example, in the simulation study, we saw team members change their rankings of candidates when they learned that their president had a different viewpoint in order to be aligned with the president. The leader of the committee can make this process more effective by setting clear norms about how the decision will be made, what each person's role is, and how the group needs to function at the very beginning of the process. Effective team leaders also help the group stick to their norms and their overarching goal during the decision-making process.

Buy-In

Using a team to make the decision helps involve team members in ensuring the chosen candidate's success. Allowing those who will be interacting with the new executive into the decision-making process—allowing them to voice their perspectives, opinions, objections, and concerns—tells them that they have a stake in the decision, whether the candidate who is actually chosen was their first choice or not.

Being a part of the selection process also affects the participants in two other ways. First, they get to evaluate all candidates and argue for the candidate they prefer. Thus, when the executive begins work, those working with him or her are already aware of the new executive's strengths and weaknesses. They have selected this executive from the other candidates because of his or her strengths and despite his or her weaknesses. If they do not take part in the decision-making process, then they may not understand why this particular executive was chosen from the pool of candidates.

Second, having been a part of the decision-making process, they also have a stake in whether the chosen executive will ultimately be a success or a failure. They will want to ensure that the decision they participated in was the right one. If those who will be working with the new executive do not participate in the selection, they will not be as motivated to ensure the success of the new executive.

Importance of Relationships

The selection process is not just about putting the right person in the right job. It is also the beginning of a relationship between the candidates and the people in the organization. In Chapter Two we reported that quality of relationships with others, especially subordinates, was among the most important criteria used to predict the success or failure of the hired executive. Furthermore, allowing the candidates to meet the executives and other employees that they will be working with gives them a chance to evaluate more realistically whether they are interested in the position and to begin planning how they will integrate into the organization.

Include Variety on the Selection Committee

Selection committees are more successful when they include executives with a variety of backgrounds and expertise. In our simulation study, human resource directors were more successful in selecting the best candidate than other high-level executives were. Presumably, they bring expertise in selection to the decision-making process; nevertheless, they were used only in one-third of the selection decisions discussed by the participants in the interview study.

Involving subordinates in the selection process tends to lead to more successful selections, but subordinates are involved in selection decisions at this level only 10 percent of the time. According to our interview study, 70 percent of the selection decisions that included input from subordinates were successful whereas only 44 percent of the selections not including subordinates were successful. Similarly, when customers (both internal and external) are involved in the selection decision, selections are also more likely to be successful. Although customers are even less likely to be included during selection of a new executive than subordinates are (7 percent of the time), when they are included the selection outcome is successful 70 percent of the time. Compare this with the 45 percent success rate of those who do not include their customers.

Subordinates and customers have a unique and valuable perspective on what the position requires. If, because of confidentiality issues, they cannot participate as decision makers, then soliciting their input is still well advised. Jon Nicholas told us, "We like to involve subordinates in a consultative approach. It is important to get a read on how the new executive is going to come across in the work group. We need to know if there are things that are really going to bother them. I've never hired anyone in my department in the last twenty years without involving subordinates."

Why does having a variety of decision makers make a positive impact on selection? Research by Benjamin Schneider at the University of Maryland and his colleagues (Schneider, Goldstein, & Smith, 1995) shows that organizations become homogeneous over time in the kinds of people in them. This is because people promote or select people to work for them who resemble themselves in many ways. The executives we spoke with were predominantly white, male, and in their mid-forties. They reported that others involved in the selection process were also white and male.

To counter the natural human bias toward similarity during selection, using "dissimilar" teams will lead to more rigorous evaluation of the candidates. Research shows that dissimilar executives pick up on different information and evaluate possible solutions differently (Melone, 1994). In addition, teams made up of executives from a variety of functional backgrounds are more likely to be creative (Williams & O'Reilly, 1998). Including a variety of executives on the team (in our case, human resource executives, subordinates, and customers) increases the variety of perspectives.

Who to Include and Who Not to Include

We found that including some executives on the selection committee is beneficial whereas including others may deter making a good selection. For example, for selections from within we found that it is useful to include the chairman of the board and peers of the new hire in the selection process. But including the entire board of directors and the "boss of the boss" decreases the chances of success.

Why is it beneficial to involve some executives and not others in high-level selections? One important factor to consider is the potential *power differential* between the members of the selection committee. Another factor is the presence of *political factions*.

Consider the Power Differential

Executives at the top of the organizational hierarchy display more assertive behaviors in meetings and other communications, speak more often, criticize more, voice more commands, and interrupt other team members more often than those lower in rank. They are given the opportunity to exert more influence, and they are evaluated more positively. Unless there are mechanisms in place to balance the power differential, the more senior executives can get their opinions out on the table for discussion and consideration, while those lower in the hierarchy have less opportunity to voice their concerns—which may be discounted anyway. In one instance in the simulation study, when the CEO stated his ranking preference of the candidates, one of the team members chimed in and looked for ways to support the CEO's ranking, even when his own original rankings had been exactly the opposite of the CEO's. He completely abandoned the important information he had obtained that could have helped the group reach a better decision.

If you are on a team where such a position power differential exists, it is important to get a clearly stated norm about what and how information will be shared before diving into the decision-making process. We often recommend that the CEO or top person hold back for the first part of the discussion to allow for a more open climate and that he or she actively encourage others to state their opinions first.

If a selection committee has a large spread in hierarchy among members, it may lead to those at the top making the choice and those lower in the hierarchy being used merely as a sounding board. Techniques of effective team process, like setting norms, listening, soliciting opinions, and periodically summarizing should be used so that everyone is encouraged to share their opinions. Another good idea is to use a skilled facilitator to enhance the team process.

Be Aware of Political Factions

Political behavior decreases the effectiveness of strategic decision making (Dean & Sharfman, 1996). Political factions are small subteams within the larger team who have different agendas or goals from the larger group agenda. When there are political factions, instead of being one united team whose goal is to make a selection, the selection committee is made up of small teams with differing subgoals. These subgoals change the process of the committee from decision making (making the best decision possible) to bargaining and negotiating (typically a win-lose orientation). Although some situations are suited to a negotiating or bargaining process, the selection process is not one of them. It is critical that all team members agree on the same agenda and goal. The team leader can facilitate this by helping the group clearly define their task and get buy-in before doing the actual decision making.

How to Choose the Selection Team

Drawing in part on the preceding discussion, we can make five suggestions to help you decide who should be involved and how to involve them in the selection process.

Design the Team for Best Results

The composition of the team affects its final decision. Therefore, selecting the selectors should not be a decision taken lightly. Include on the selection committee a variety of people who will be working with the new hire, such as the new executive's superior, human resource directors, subordinates, customers, peers, and members of teams that the new hire will be joining. At the same time, keep the selection committee as small as possible. In our research, we found that most selection committees included four or five key members. Other executives who are not given direct decision-making responsibility can be introduced to the candidates in the candidate pool and allowed to voice their opinions.

Take Team Dynamics into Account

It is especially important to consider the effects of hierarchy, politics, and conflict on team members. Intentionally choose people who have demonstrated their ability to put aside their own agendas for the good of the organization and their willingness to listen to diverse viewpoints. We have seen executives with certain biases about the best choice who solidify their position before coming into the team discussion. The team process thus becomes one of looking for allies and coalitions rather than getting all the information on the table to make the most informed choice. For example, one hiring committee we worked with contained two factions with two completely different views of what the organization needed. One faction was attracted to candidates with strong financial expertise; the other faction was attracted to candidates with easygoing and laid-back styles. This team was unable to come to a satisfactory decision. We have also seen team members allow information to be misinterpreted by the team if it benefited their own chosen candidate. In these cases a poor-quality decision was the result of a failed team process. We saw this frequently in the simulation study.

For your selection committee you will want people who can put the needs of the organization first, can come to decision making with an open mind, and have good conflict resolution and listening skills.

Explicitly frame the task and the norms of the decision-making team at the beginning so that all of them are clear about their roles and their task. Norms can identify openness and listening as clearly expected behaviors. Stipulate at the beginning how the decision will be made (for example, using consensus, vote, recommendations to someone else, or input only). Teams are much more likely to make successful choices if members listen to each other, are open to differing opinions, do not simply advocate for their own choice, are willing to share and correct information, and establish neutral candidate requirements. The members of one team we observed during the simulation decided not to reveal who their individual choices were. They spent a lot of time assessing the needs of the organization and developing the candidate criteria as a team. Their performance was so good that it looked as if they had read the correct solution before undertaking the decision-making process.

Spell Out Responsibilities of the Selection Committee

Mel Sorcher in his classic book *Predicting Executive Success* (1985) suggests that those who make the selection decision have six responsibilities:

- Ensuring that the search mechanisms or processes develop a sufficient number of candidates.

- Ensuring that the candidates identified possess the required characteristics and experience.

- Ensuring that the committee looks deep enough within the organization for candidates.

- Deciding whether to promote from within or hire from the outside.

- Keeping an open mind and getting advice from others outside the immediate committee.
- Holding a minority opinion, even if others on the committee agree on a candidate.

Make a Team-Based Decision

To make the selection decision, using a consultative style (asking others for their opinions but having one individual responsible for making the final decision) or using team consensus (allowing the team to make the decision) are both viable options. In either case, using a team is the best way to ensure that range and accuracy are included, buy-in is created, and relationships are established prior to the actual selection choice.

Use the Same Decision Makers
Throughout the Decision Process

Avoid the problem described by one executive, who told us, "Different executive-level employees interviewed different candidates, so nobody could compare." *All* decision makers should have equal access to the entire selection process discussed in the next several chapters.

Summary

In this chapter, we emphasized the importance of carefully considering which people will have the responsibility of making the selection decision. Teams, used either in a consultative manner or to make the decision themselves, are more likely to choose a successful executive because they have a greater range and accuracy of information, are more likely to buy in to the selected candidate, and can begin developing relationships with the candidate who is ultimately chosen. One caveat we noted is that all the decision makers should have equal access to the entire selection process.

Using subgroups for different tasks can actually prevent a team from working effectively.

Having a variety of executives on the selection committee is associated with making a successful selection. We also found that human resource executives, subordinates, and customers all can be helpful in the decision-making process. But when a variety of people are included, it is important to be aware of the problems of power differentials, political factions, and other team dynamics. Be prepared to deal with these issues early in the process by setting norms and clearly spelling out responsibilities, or consider using a skilled facilitator.

In the next chapter, we will see that the first task that the selection committee must accomplish is to pool together accurate information about the organization's needs, the position requirements, and the candidate requirements. Although this task tends to be difficult, tedious, and time consuming, it is crucial to the success of the selection process.

Chapter Four

Mapping the Selection Challenge

To find the best candidate for a position, successful selectors take a systematic, disciplined, and context-rich look at the organization and its environment, the open position, and the candidate requirements. They look first at the organization's needs, its strategy, and how a particular position helps implement the strategy, and only then do they go on to define candidate requirements.

For years, industrial and organizational psychologists, search firms, and organizational experts have been proclaiming the importance of determining what is needed in the organization and the position before embarking on the executive selection process. Yet today's executives show little inclination to analyze organizational needs and position requirements before filling an open executive position. This lack of clarity can have a dramatic impact on the success of the selection. As one executive who hired an unsuccessful executive reflected, "More time should be spent on job definition and less on selection." Others have said that the "good old boy" method of promotion is not nearly as effective as systems that take a much more objective approach.

Successful selectors we interviewed indicated that they were more explicit in defining organizational needs, position requirements, and candidate requirements than unsuccessful selectors were. The successful selectors made such statements as, "I felt that the selection went well because all the homework had been done. The position was spelled out and the characteristics needed were well defined." Our data show that successful selectors were more specific.

Preparation has four objectives. It aims to ensure that pertinent information is considered, different perspectives are heard, there is an understanding of what this particular executive will be expected to do, and all of those involved (including the decision makers, the candidates, and those who will be assessing the executive's performance) are in agreement about what they are looking for and why.

Preparation includes three general steps: *identifying the needs of the organization*, *identifying the position requirements*, and *identifying the candidate requirements*.

Step 1: Identify the Needs of the Organization

An effective assessment of the organization and its strategy is the linchpin in the successful selection outcome. Those who hire successfully do a better organizational needs assessment than those who do not. A typical comment about a successful selection was this: "We used the vision-mission of the company to define this position." Those who were not successful tended to say, "There was a gap between what the company said and believed it needed versus what it really needed. Therefore, there was not a match between the person hired and the business needs."

Why is it important to assess organizational needs before selecting an executive? The organizational environment has an impact on selection at the top—whether the issues are made clear or not (Sessa & Campbell, 1997). All the executives involved in the selection process have their own views of the organization. For example, some of them may concentrate on the company's long-term goals and values, whereas others may think that the issue of utmost concern is this quarter's balance sheet. Some may believe that the future of the organization is in mergers and acquisitions, others may concentrate on quality and brand loyalty, others may be concerned with technological improvements, others may think that developing the next generation of leaders is the top issue, and still others may just want to hire someone they will enjoy working with. Often selection is a result of each executive's own projections onto the particular set of candidates.

If these issues are not gotten out into the open and resolved, chaos may result. Executives will search for candidates who "fit" their various definitions of what the organization needs. Subsequently, they will be stunned to find that every other executive involved in the selection committee has a totally different lineup of candidates based on a different set of needs.

Common Organizational Needs

A sampling of what the executives in our interview study mentioned in general as organizational needs includes these: sustaining the organization (63 percent), growing the organization (21 percent), handling a turnaround situation (20 percent), handling a start-up initiative (19 percent), managing cultural or strategic change (18 percent), and restructuring (17 percent).

Critical Conditions

Having an understanding of organizational needs is critical to fulfilling its strategy. However, some particular strategic objectives are much more difficult to attain than others. Three specific complex organizational conditions require special attention in the selection process: *mergers or acquisitions, cultural or strategic changes,* and *start-up situations.* (See Table 4.1.)

Mergers or Acquisitions. We found that the highest risk condition for any new executive is merger or acquisition. Executives hired into organizations undergoing a merger or acquisition show a 69 percent failure rate (or 31 percent success rate).

During a merger or acquisition the criteria for success are amorphous and ambiguous. These are times of upheaval for companies. Cultures are being mingled. Values are clashing. Functions are

Table 4.1 Critical Organizational Needs at the Time of Hiring.

Organizational Condition	Number of Executives Mentioning	Percentage of Successful Hires
Merger or acquisition Internal and external hires combined	29	31
Cultural or strategic change		
Internal hires	23	65
External hires	34	41
Start-up		
Internal hires	8	63
External hires	26	33

Note: N = 321; internal = 149; external = 172
Source: Sessa, Kaiser, Taylor, & Campbell, 1998.

being consolidated. There are winners and losers in the battle for consolidated positions. Emotions run high. Decisions seem arbitrary. Employees are stressed, angry, worn out.

What does this mean for those executives who are selected either to manage the merger or acquisition or to participate in it? Their job is by definition a difficult one. They must mastermind the joining of two companies—a challenging job in itself. At the same time, these executives must deal with the stress of the change both for themselves and for their employees. Whether the merger or acquisition ultimately goes smoothly or not, the executives involved are held responsible for any mishaps occurring along the way. In addition, once the change is made the survivors sometimes perceive that the executive is no longer needed or is unable to adjust to the "stability" of the new organization. He or she is now seen as a failure.

Cultural or Strategic Change. A second high-risk condition for a new hire is during cultural or strategic change. When the organization's culture or strategy is changing, it is hard to define effective results. The process is delicate and difficult. The old way of doing things is no longer appropriate yet is deeply ingrained in the organization and holds a powerful unconscious influence on all behavior. The new way of doing and being is not yet clear.

Though the success rate of those hired from outside the organization under these conditions is moderate, our research indicates that those promoted from within are more likely to be successful. Why is this true? External executives are usually brought in because they have had different experiences and therefore have a range of new ideas to implement. But they are at a serious disadvantage because they are not familiar with the current culture or acquainted with the current way of doing things. Moreover, they do not know the employees and have not built supportive relationships. Having someone arrive from the outside and immediately make changes, or even slowly make changes, may cause employees to be resentful, distrustful, and resistant. For example, one of our executives said, "He restructured the department without getting information on ownership from those with tenure in the department." External executives are therefore in a bind. They have been told during the hiring process that they are being hired for their outside perspective. They feel that to prove their worth, they need to begin making changes immediately. They end up being seen as critical, thinking they have all the right answers. This can make them seem insensitive and arrogant.

Although executives promoted from inside the company may have a narrower range of innovative ideas, they have a better understanding of what would and would not work in the organization. Coming from inside the organization, they do not need to learn the current culture while changing to the new one. They know what works well and what needs to be changed. They also know the employees and executives, including those who support their ideas and those who do not. This makes the changes they make less hazardous and the employees less resistant.

Start-Up Situation. A third difficult organizational condition for a new hire to deal with is the start-up of a new business unit. Executives hired to be involved in a start-up are usually expected to act on their own. They are given carte blanche or are loosely supervised. One of the selectors in our interview study gave a good example of this process with the following statement: "The typical process when starting up a company in a new country [is] they select an experienced corporation guy, give him a bag of money and total freedom, and send him to the new country." Although start-up executives are involved in making their mark on the company, they are also dealing with political, social, and cultural dilemmas beyond the job itself.

As Table 4.1 shows, organizations usually hire external executives to handle these positions. Intuitively, this makes sense, but our research suggests that internal hires have a 63 percent success rate whereas external hires have only a 33 percent success rate in start-up situations. Why are internal executives more likely to succeed in this environment? As when dealing with cultural or strategic change, it may be that critical skills for this sort of position have more to do with political, social, and cultural dilemmas of working in the organization than dealing with the start-up itself.

Internal executives are already high on the learning curve, particularly when it comes to organizational sensitivities, compared with those hired from the outside. They have already succeeded in their organization. They know the employees and those they can depend on, they know the culture, they know what is acceptable and what is not, and they have their networks—both formal and informal—already established. People hired from the outside may have the skills, expertise, and experience needed to succeed, but they must do so in a situation they know very little about. They receive little supervision, they do not know the skills of others or the people they can depend on, they do not know the "proper" manner of doing things in the company. They are clearly at a disadvantage, no matter whether the start-up itself is ultimately successful or not. In these cases, paying particular attention to helping the external candidate assimilate is important.

Issues to Consider in Assessing the Organization

An organizational assessment begins with the organization's overall strategy, its culture, its competitive environment, and its short- and long-term goals. To operate effectively, most organizations already have this information. The challenge is to make it relevant to each separate executive selection. The easiest way to accomplish this is to bring together the selection committee (as well as any knowledgeable others whose ideas should be considered) to discuss questions such as the following:

- What do our vision, our strategy, our goals, and our structure say we need?

- How does our organization do things and how do we want to do things in the future? What does this say we need in hiring a new executive?

- What do we value?

- How are we unique?

- What are our biggest issues going to be in the next few years? Experts (for example, see Hesselbein, Goldsmith, & Beckhard, 1996; Kurtzman, 1998; McFarland, Senn, & Childress, 1993) believe companies need to pay attention to globalization; increased competition; economic, political, and social upheaval; alliances, joint ventures, and partnerships; flatter organizations; management of processes (instead of units or people); learning organizations; and temporary employees.

- Where are we weak, and do we want to improve in these areas?

- Where are we strong, and do we want to be even stronger in these areas?

- What are our climate, culture, and leadership styles?
- What kind of person do we want to work with?
- What kind of person would enjoy working here, would do well in this sort of environment?
- What does it mean to be successful in this organization?

Step 2: Identify the Position Requirements

The next step is to determine the actual requirements of the position. Those who do a superficial assessment of position requirements are less likely to be successful than those who do a more in-depth and specific assessment. Those who hire an unsuccessful executive are later likely to say such things as, "Requirements for this position were not written down until three to four months after the individual had been hired and was beginning to be unsuccessful." Or, "The VP originally defined the position but the job description did not fit the job. Therefore, a true assessment was not really made and not much time was spent on it."

Why is it important to assess position requirements? You may be asking, "Shouldn't the new executive define the position?" Or you may be thinking, "The job changes daily. By the time we define it, it will be completely different." These are both valid points. However, we argue that it is important to ensure that those who are making the selection, the executive accepting the position, and the people who ultimately will be assessing performance have a clear idea of how the executive will be judged once in the position. For those making the decision, knowing the position requirements helps when differentiating between candidates. For executives accepting the position, it allows them to have a realistic idea of what will be expected in the position and clear goals once in the position. For those who then assess the executive, the position requirements help to determine whether and how well the new hire has accomplished the job.

Common Position Requirements

A sampling of what the executives in our interview study mentioned in general as position requirements include these: developing strategy (47 percent), accomplishing tasks specific to a department (42 percent), managing or supervising people (37 percent), improving business or productivity (31 percent), charting new directions (27 percent), building, maintaining, or participating in a team (26 percent), and developing a vision (19 percent).

We found that when position requirements are framed in such statements as "improving business or productivity" or "developing employees," the candidate selected was likely to be ultimately unsuccessful. In contrast, when job requirements included such statements as "maintaining ethics" and "fixing a political situation," the executive selected was likely to be ultimately successful. And when job requirements included "charting new directions," internal candidates fared better than external candidates. Although these correlations might seem odd at first, at second glance they make a lot of sense. The underlying differences have to do with specificity (ethics, political situations) versus generality (improving business or productivity).

"Improving business or productivity" is a general goal that is open to many interpretations and may be addressed through many different methods. What *improvement* means to one executive may be very different from what it means to another. For example, how much does the business or productivity need to improve to be recognized as accomplishment of the goal? What if radical change, which leads to lower productivity for a short time, needs to be instituted before improvement can occur? What if the executive does improve the business or productivity, but others don't like how he or she does it? How long does the improvement have to be sustained (knowing as we do that improvement is based in part on factors beyond any executive's control)? One quarter? One year? Even longer? Executives are typically given six months before their success is measured. The goal of improving business or productivity can be made more specific if more parameters are outlined and all executives know and are in agreement about what those parameters are.

Position requirements such as "maintaining ethics" and "fixing a political situation" are more specific and consequently result in more successful hires. Here, there is a recognition that something in the organization needs to be changed. The top-level executives have defined it and can specifically look for information on the candidates regarding how they would handle the situation.

In contrast, like the first set of requirements, the requirement to "develop employees" is also linked to failure. Interestingly, although organizations were more likely to look outside when they believed that their own employees needed to be developed, executives hired from the outside were not likely to be successful. And those hired from inside the organization were seen as successful only half the time. This is a particularly difficult situation for an organization to be in. It recognizes that it does not have the bench strength to ensure its survival, and it also recognizes that one of the requirements needed in the position is to develop systems that improve its people. However, this may be a problem that cannot be solved by one individual but rather must be solved in another manner. For example, top management may need to make a concerted effort to develop or improve on a succession plan and implement training. Developing employees is a long-term process. Nevertheless, even here, the success rate of new hires may be improved if the job parameters are made more specific. For example, state that the new hire should develop a succession plan and create development processes with a view toward long-term outcomes.

One last difficult and complicated position requirement is to "chart new directions." Interestingly, when this particular position requirement is an issue, those promoted from within are more likely to be successful than those hired from the outside. Relationships and organizational knowledge are as critical here as the ability to chart change. Having a known track record, having relationships with key executives, and understanding organizational support and the political framework are critical in charting change. External hires, who must learn the organization at the same time they are charting new directions, have a formidable task.

Issues to Consider in Defining Position Requirements

Figuring out position requirements at the top three levels of the organization is problematic. Separating the job from the person in the job is difficult, as is defining exactly what is meant by being successful at it.

When defining position requirements, use internal expertise and be specific. The executive currently in the position, his or her superiors, peers in similar positions, the team with whom the new hire will be working, and subordinates all have knowledge about what outcomes will be needed. The goal is to get a good description of where the position is today and approximately where the organization wants the position to go. A newly hired senior executive can help refine the specifics of where the organization wants to go and the best route to get there—that's part of the expertise he or she will bring.

Ask such questions as these:

- *What are the goals of this position?* Make sure you consider all the organizational needs previously listed to ensure that any that are directly related to this position are considered.

- *What are the major tasks and activities?* Include both "work" and "people-management" tasks and activities.

- *How does this position relate to other positions?* Is there anything in particular to keep in mind about the person who is currently in the position (for example, working style)?

- *What are the strengths of this team or department?* Does this position require the executive to have these strengths as well?

- *What are the weaknesses of this team or department?* What does this position need to help rectify these weaknesses?

- *What will it mean to be successful in this position?* Think about organizational results, relationships, and performance issues, as discussed in Chapter Two. Such criteria should be spelled out as carefully as possible because they can be used to evaluate the new hire.

Step 3: Identify the Candidate Requirements

Only at this point is it time to describe the candidate requirements. Unfortunately, our research shows us that this is the point at which most organizations *begin* the selection process. Executives are comfortable and articulate when describing what they need in an executive. They begin by listing such things as functional backgrounds and specific experiences, knowledge, skills, abilities, and personal characteristics. But these are seldom explicitly linked to the organization's analysis and position requirements.

Successful selectors are more likely to do a more in-depth and specific assessment of candidates. Executives who hire a successful executive actually list more candidate requirements than those who hire an unsuccessful executive. Those who hire an unsuccessful executive are later apt to say such things as, "We left values and temperament out of the assessment" or "Given Gil's background, his strengths didn't fit the profile of what the board thought was necessary to get the job done" (Bournellis, 1997, p. 7). In contrast, those who hire a successful executive indicate that they learned through experience the importance of doing this preparation. For example: "Our candidate requirements were quite explicit because we had come close to hiring someone whom we very much liked but who probably did not meet the requirements for the job. It was this that prompted us to very explicitly list the job criteria and the candidate requirements."

Why is it important to detail candidate requirements? As with the organizational analysis and the position requirements, the primary purpose for outlining candidate requirements is to develop a clear set of expectations among everyone involved in the selection process. For example, if all agree that a new vision is needed to drive this portion of the organization forward and that this position will be one of three positions charged with developing that vision, then candidate requirements might include having experience in creating a vision, having good ideas about where this company should go, and having the ability to work in teams.

Common Candidate Requirements

In general, candidate requirements fall into three categories: *hardside requirements, soft-side requirements,* and *fit.* (See Table 4.2.)

Hard-side requirements are tangible and measurable; they are a person's credentials and achievements. Soft-side requirements are matters of style, personality, and culture. Fit requires a special explanation. Although finding an executive who "fits" is the goal of the selection process, it is also the ultimate inferential attribute. Fit is the perceived similarity among the persons making the selection decision, the organization, the position, and the executive applying for the position. Those who fit are liked by other executives. Those who do not fit are not liked (Judge & Ferris, 1992). Despite the subjectivity of fit, it wouldn't be acceptable to select people you don't know, don't feel comfortable with, and with whom you have poor chemistry. In contrast, if fit is used as a justification for not hiring "nontypical" executives (for example, on the basis of religion, ethnicity, or gender) then that is unfair bias. One executive described to us an all-male team meeting at his company's executive hunting lodge. They raucously enjoyed after-dinner liqueurs and cigars while examining the guns that had been issued to them for the next day's hunt. This team bemoaned the fact that they had no women in their executive ranks, but at the same time they reveled in the fact that they had such a high level of camaraderie and so little conflict. They were all so much alike that they could not see that perhaps this culture was unfriendly to

Table 4.2 Candidate Requirements.

Candidate Requirements	Percentage of Executives Mentioning
Hard-Side Requirements	
Specific functional background	62
Technical knowledge	35
Specific task skills	24
Intensive experience in a field	23
Specific degrees	22
Intensive experience in an industry	21
Specific business experience	20
Industry knowledge	12
Job knowledge	12
Soft-Side Requirements	
Skills:	
Managerial	43
Interpersonal	39
Communication	37
Leadership	33
Strategic planning	16
Characteristics:	
Team player	31
Ethical	18
Energetic, driven	17
Intelligent	16
Flexible	15
Creative	15
Fit	
Company knowledge	17
Fit with culture	16

Note: N = 319

Source: Sessa, Kaiser, Taylor, & Campbell, 1998.

women. One might wonder how much "fit" in this organization depended on being comfortable in a smoke-filled room with a group of guys getting ready for a hunt.

Critical Issues

As with organizational needs and position requirements, there are some critical issues to keep in mind when delineating candidate requirements.

Specificity Versus Generality. We found that successful selectors were more specific in defining candidate requirements than were unsuccessful selectors. They listed such requirements as dedication, ethics, fit with the culture, creativity, and interpersonal skills. Unsuccessful selectors were more likely to list such broad requirements as "management skills." Once again, the key to success here is clarifying the requirements rather than leaving them in broad, ambiguous terms that may mean different things to different selectors.

Internal Versus External Selections. When candidate requirements include fit with the culture, intensive experience in a particular field, flexibility and adaptability, or relevant job knowledge, hires from within are more likely to be successful than hires from outside the organization.

When fit to the culture is particularly important it comes as no surprise that those who are hired from the inside are more likely to be seen as successful. But what about when experience in a particular field, flexibility or adaptability, or relevant job knowledge is needed? It is much easier for the executives to assess these qualities over a long period of time and in a less formal setting than during a short selection process. Evidence shows that those who fit the organization are more likely to remain with the organization than those who do not (Schneider, Goldstein, & Smith, 1995). Assessing fit of an external candidate over a short period of time (that is, during the selection process) is difficult and fraught with potential error.

Flexibility, adaptability, and job knowledge are also difficult to assess in outsiders. For these qualities, selectors are forced to rely on asking both the candidate and references if they think the candidate has the needed requirements. However, a person who is flexible in one environment may not be flexible in another. Job knowledge and experience in a particular field may also be situation-specific.

Issues to Consider in Defining Candidate Requirements

Developing a list of relevant candidate requirements requires translating objective, measurable organizational needs and position requirements into measurable executive requirements. This is not easy to do. It is one thing to say that you need to restructure the organization to consolidate product lines while globalizing your market strategy (organization assessment and job requirement). It is quite another to determine what skills and characteristics in a person can best produce those outcomes. Does this person absolutely have to have managed a restructuring in the past? What other experiences, knowledge, skills, and abilities could substitute? The critical variable in defining candidate requirements is specifically linking the candidate requirements to the organizational needs and position requirements.

Questions to ask include these:

- What experiential or background requirements derive from our organizational needs and job requirements?
- What knowledge, skills, abilities, or characteristics are needed to do the work? To survive in our organization?
- What are the educational requirements? Are degrees or licenses needed?
- Have the selectors considered the need for the following candidate characteristics (as suggested by contemporary leadership experts): vision, wisdom, courage, trust, mentoring skills, risk-taking behavior, decisiveness, charisma, links with the outside world, broad view?

- What do executives need to have in order to be successful in this organization?

There Is No Perfect Candidate

One of our clients told us about his company's idea of the perfect selection process: "We not only want someone who can walk on water, but we need someone who can predict that they can walk on water!" Assessing all of the relevant requirements in every candidate would make the selection process a nightmare. The key to a successful selection process is to discuss what is needed in this candidate for this particular organization and position *and* to make sure the selection committee agrees on the most important requirements, thus avoiding problems like those of the executive who told us this: "The candidate requirements were clearly known to me, but I probably didn't communicate them clearly." With over thirty years of assessment data on leaders at the Center for Creative Leadership, we can tell you that there is no perfect leader—all selections are a trade-off. The key is to know what qualities are most important.

Once the important candidate requirements are defined, the next step is to determine which of the requirements are absolutely necessary for an executive to be successful, which ones would be useful if you can find them, and which are specifications that the organization could work around if necessary. Most important, the selection committee needs to come to agreement on the three to five must-haves to ensure success in the position. They need to be willing to discuss the trade-offs and stand behind their choice. Remember, no one walks on water. What are your trade-offs and are you willing to stand behind those choices? Stan Horner, Director of Executive Education at Dell Computers, told us, "Dell puts a high priority on carefully selecting executives based on fourteen key competencies that track with hard measures of performance. Five of these competencies are things that are hard to develop, like integrity. The other nine vary in importance depending on the job. Dell is very intentional about selecting executives that clearly meet the competencies for that particular job." Similarly, Jon Nicholas of Maytag told us that he sorts the company's twenty key competencies into three piles for each job: must-haves, nice-to-haves, and luxuries.

Summary

We have covered a lot of material in this chapter. And the work we have discussed is difficult, even tedious. But we believe that spending the time—even the majority of selection time—on these issues will make the rest of the selection process go much more smoothly. The three key steps of conducting an organizational needs assessment, outlining position requirements, and outlining candidate requirements together define what to look for in a potential candidate and how to determine if the new executive is ultimately successful once in the position. The clearer you are in carrying out these three steps, the more successful the selection is likely to be. If you skip these three steps, the rest of the selection process is merely ritual.

Why? The main reason is that all executives involved—including the one who is ultimately selected—need to have a clear and shared idea of what is expected. Not having a clear and shared perspective results in flawed decision making. In contrast, if you take the three steps described here, you will have the opportunity to ensure that all important information is considered, different perspectives are brought out and heard, there is understanding and a common language for describing what the hired executive is expected to be able to accomplish, and everyone involved is in agreement. In sum, all the executives involved will have created a picture or impression of an ideal candidate that they all agree on. This picture will serve as the guide for the rest of the process. It will be used continually during the selection process. It will be used as a communication device in recruiting a candidate pool, as a mechanism to assess fit during the selection decision, and as a tool both to help guide new hires in their work and to determine if they are successful once they are on the job.

In the next chapter, we will show that although putting together accurate information about the organization, the position, and the candidate requirements is important, the task is far from over. The organization must also do a good job of attracting quality talent. Insufficient and inaccurate information makes a good decision impossible, but not having quality candidates to choose among can make even the best information useless!

Chapter Five

Attracting Quality Talent

A good selection process is useless if there is no talent pool to select from. In a perfect world organizations could choose a candidate from a pool of highly qualified individuals, all capable of being successful. In reality, selection committees often have only one candidate with some of the qualifications they are looking for while the rest of the candidates fall short. Most executives we interviewed find their talent pools distressingly small.

Why is it important to develop a good candidate pool? Without a pool of qualified executives, the best selection practices in the world will not work. Potential candidates set the upper limit on the effectiveness of the selection process. To recruit the best executive for the position, you must attract the best. The best candidate may come from inside the organization (through executive development, succession plans, or other internal networks) or outside the organization (either within the industry or outside it, through such sources as consultants, word of mouth, and advertisements).

The executives we interviewed told us that they chose a particular candidate because he or she was either the only candidate under consideration or because the others were lacking something. Nearly a quarter of the time the executive selected for the position was the only candidate considered.

The president of a major division of a Fortune 100 company told us about the latest selection of a CEO of his company. He noted that when the current CEO announced his intention to retire, there was one viable candidate for that position. This one person had been the designated heir for at least ten years. Although this individual was very competent, he had a narrow range of experience. Yet, as with many companies, the business climate had changed dramatically over that ten-year time period to a more competitive and international one. This CEO wished that the company had had a larger pool of candidates to select from who were better prepared for operating in a bigger world.

Recent data from a McKinsey & Co. study support the need for broadening the talent pool, finding that three-quarters of the top-level executives they surveyed said their companies had insufficient talent or were chronically short of talent. Only 23 percent of the executives surveyed strongly agreed that their companies attract highly talented people, and just 10 percent said that they retain almost all of their high performers (Chambers, Foulon, Handfield-Jones, Hankin, & Michaels, 1998).

Knowledge is limited on this very important step in the selection process. In the social and behavioral sciences, research on recruitment into the executive ranks is scant—organizations with successful processes often do not reveal their methods, and executive search firms have not shared their techniques with the public in ways that allow us to develop a knowledge base about recruiting at executive levels. But we do know that it is important to think about recruitment from the organizational point of view *and* from the applicant's point of view.

The Organizational Point of View

During recruitment, the goal of the organization is to communicate the nature of the organization (its culture, for example), the nature of the position opening, and the qualifications to possible applicants inside and outside the organization. If the applicants feel that there is a match between what they have to offer and what the organization needs, and if the offer appears attractive to them, they will put themselves into the candidate pool. The goal of the organization is *not* to attract a maximum number of candidates but rather to attract a select number of highly qualified candidates. Basically, organizations are "marketing to a niche audience."

The organization and the position need to appear positive: the organization needs to show both why it is an excellent one to work for and why this particular position is interesting and challenging. This kind of advertising may be conveyed through carefully crafted organizational materials. But it is important to remember that it is also conveyed through every encounter potential candidates have with the organization—from newspaper headlines about the company to Wall Street hype to communication with representatives of the organization.

Appearing positive is not enough. The organization also needs to usher applicants into the process in a way that engenders realistic expectations. Applicants need information that allows them to decide whether this particular position and this particular organization is suitable or a good fit for them. An executive at one company told us, "We encourage applicants to openly ask questions about the culture. We want to give them as realistic a picture as we possibly can." The organizational psychology literature describes this as giving a *realistic job preview*. A realistic job preview gives potential candidates enough information to allow them to evaluate whether they would fit well in the organization and position. This is important in promoting the eventual success of the hired executive. Those executives who have a realistic picture of the position and organization before accepting an offer are more likely to have higher job performance and are less likely to leave, either voluntarily or involuntarily (Phillips, 1998; Bauer, Morrison, & Callister, 1998).

Finally, the organization needs to present information that distinguishes it and the position opening from other possible organizations and positions. What makes this organization and this position interesting, unique, appealing? How will this position have a real impact on the future of the organization?

Thus, during the recruitment stage of the selection process, the organization is in both a marketing and an advertising mode.

Potential qualified and interested applicants are the customers. The organization and the applicants are entering into a negotiating relationship. Although particular executives may not choose to join the pool of candidates at this time, or may not be deemed appropriate to do so, it is to the organization's advantage to treat them all in such a manner that they feel positive about their encounter with the organization and the people in it.

The Applicant's Point of View

Recruitment is largely about self-selection into a candidate pool. Rarely do uninterested parties apply for a position. Thus, a useful way to view the recruitment of a candidate pool is through the eyes of the potential applicant. Along with being a "customer" of the selection process, applicants are also negotiating and developing a relationship with the organization.

As we stated in the preceding section, applicants need to get enough information to decide if they are interested in a position. But they need more than that. First, their emotions need to be taken into account. The entire selection process can cause anxiety in potential candidates. They need to be kept informed about what stage the selection process is in and what their standing is. They need to hear this information from enthusiastic, informative, and credible organization representatives. Unimpressive or offensive procedures not only will turn qualified current applicants off but also will have a negative impact on future hiring processes.

Second, as already stated, applicants need a realistic idea of the position. What executives expect from their new positions is usually different from the reality. New executives generally have higher expectations of the amount of responsibility, intellectual challenge, use of abilities, degree of training, and management attention than they ultimately find when they are hired. The greater the discrepancy between expectations and reality, the lower the executive's satisfaction and commitment and the higher the chance of turnover down the line (Mabey & Iles, 1991).

Third, candidates need to know who they will be working for and with as well as who will be working for them. They can thus assess whether they will fit with the people they will be working with and the organizational culture. As we saw in Chapter Three, it is beneficial to introduce candidates to their subordinates and customers, superior, peers, team members, and others with whom they will be working. Relationships can start developing as early as the first encounter between a candidate and potential coworkers.

Spreading the Net

Effective recruitment promotes candidate success (Rynes, Orlitzky, & Bretz, 1997). For a candidate pool to develop, both internal and external candidates must be made aware of the position opening. There are five viable options for advertising a position opening: *succession plans, nominations, advertisements, research,* and *executive search firms.* Depending on the circumstances, you may choose to use one, several, or all five options in your search.

Succession Plans

The first possible source of high-quality candidates is the firm's own succession plan, if it has one. In our interview study, only 15 percent of the candidates selected for the position were from the succession plan! This is surprising, because there is a growing interest in and development of succession planning in organizations. Our findings indicate that internal candidates are often more successful than external candidates (see Chapter Eight), so the development and use of a well-thought-out succession plan is important.

Extensive use of succession planning is a fairly recent phenomenon. One senior executive told us that his company had identified several strategic needs: selling a bundle of products, being more integrated as a company, and moving into international business. He worked with human resources to think about critical skill sets necessary in a top-level executive to lead these strategies, and then went on to develop a detailed succession plan. The company's problem was that this process was less than two years old, so the people it was then considering for very senior positions had not had the benefit of this kind of developmental experience. In the future, we may see more impact from succession planning.

Nominations from Knowledgeable Others

Asking for nominations from executives who have a vested interest in or some connection to the organization is a good way to begin developing a list of potential candidates to contact, even though those asked often answer the question immediately without giving it much thought. Nevertheless, good candidates, or individuals not usually thought of, can come to your attention in this manner.

A more fruitful way to get nominations is directly through a search committee. The executives on the search team probably have many candidates in mind, both internal and external, whom they think would be good. Now is the time to get all of those names on the potential contact list.

Networking to create a continual pool of candidates is an important part of any executive's job. It is not a good idea to turn on the candidate "spigot" only when a position is opening. The best chance for finding really good people comes from constant networking and from positive contacts created when recruiting for previous positions. One very big mistake that executives make is thinking that they must start over with each new position.

One company president told us, "I am always on a talent search. You might even say I am a talent junkie. I always want to know what talent is out there." It is worth the time it takes to build relationships with people who were considered for one job but were not found to be the "right fit" if they are talented. Make sure that their phone calls are returned personally, that they are given clear reasons for why they were not selected for this particular position, and that they are told why the company is still interested. Then, stay in touch with them. Relationships with talented people are built over time. And when there is an opening, a much greater choice among potential candidates is available.

Advertisements

Placing advertisements in the appropriate professional journals, newspapers, on the Web, and through in-house job posting systems is also a way to develop names for the candidate pool. The key word here is *appropriate*. *The Wall Street Journal*, *The New York Times*, and other trade and professional publications have limited circulations and may not be read by many potential candidates—particularly those who are not middle-aged, white, and male. Advertisements need to be placed where minorities and women will also see them. The resulting responses are self-nominated. However, although this option may lead to a large volume of potential candidates, the quality may be uneven.

Research

In 1989, Garrison suggested that one of the most productive sources for nominations is good basic research. In most industries and professions some institutions are considered to be premier: most successful, prestigious, and productive. The search committee can proactively look at these organizations and their top management for outstanding or unique individuals. If you consider your organization to be at the pinnacle in its area, then ensure that your internal candidates are given the same scrutiny and attention that is being given to other top-notch executives.

Executive Search Firms

An alternative to doing the research yourself is to contract with a search firm to do it. Use of executive search firms in the United States and around the world is increasing. Search professionals have two clients. First, they aid organizations in conducting the search. They may help a company define the position and what they want in a candidate and provide a candidate pool. Second, search professionals consider individual executives to be clients, aiding them in finding positions that match their knowledge, skills, abilities, and desires. Search professionals also act as an intermediary between the organization and the executive, helping with negotiations, advising each client how to act, and offering other help as situations require.

The role of executive search professionals varies depending on the wants of the organization retaining them. At minimum, executive search professionals help clients find a suitable number of potential candidates. At maximum, a professional can manage the entire search process from conducting the organizational analysis to following up with the candidate after placement.

There are several benefits to using search firms. First, they have the expertise and the time to do the research. Second, they have contacts and résumé banks that can generate serious candidates fast. And third, they can provide an objective third-party view of the process.

There are also a number of difficulties when you use a search firm. They vary in quality, and unless careful attention is paid and time spent on selecting the right search firm, the entire selection process will not be successful. In addition, there are few descriptions of how executive searchers actually conduct executive searches. David DeVries (1993) suggests that there is reason to believe these firms rely too much on picking candidates who fit into the culture and less on who will be approved by the decision makers. Finally, search firms are outside contractors. Although they may be able to find a pool of qualified candidates, they cannot and should not take the place of an internal search committee that knows the organization, its needs, and makes the final selection decision.

If you decide to use a search firm to aid in the development of the candidate pool, it is crucial that the firm research all candidates including the ones you have found on your own and any internal candidates you are considering. In addition, you will enhance your success if you are clear with the search firm about the organizational needs, the position requirements, and the critical candidate requirements. In the next chapter we explain why it is much easier for the selection committee to compare executives when they have comparable information on each. Having in-depth reports prepared by search firms on some candidates and other kinds of information on other candidates leads to confusion and possibly bias.

Executives at Maytag feel that using a search firm has been very helpful to them. However, they have chosen to use one firm exclusively so that all of the search firm staff know the Maytag managers well and have contact with a wide variety of people in the company.

Putting Variety into the Candidate Pool

Once executives begin to express interest in being considered for a position, the questions for the search committee become, "Who should we consider?" and "How many should we consider?" One important finding that we uncovered in our research is that the key to a good candidate pool is variety. As we have noted in the previous chapters, the typical top executive selected in today's organizations is white (93 percent), middle-aged (average age forty-two), and male (86 percent), much as typical top executives have been in the past (see Sessa & Campbell, 1997). The pool from which the selected candidate is typically drawn is also predominantly white, middle-aged, and male.

Having top-quality nontraditional candidates in the candidate pool may be beneficial. Although the numbers were small in our sample, selected nonwhite executives were more likely to be seen as successful than unsuccessful, whereas selected white executives were found to have a fifty-fifty shot at success.

The proportion of internal to external candidates is also important. We found that the candidate pools of companies whose internal selection proved successful contained more external candidates than did the candidate pools of companies whose internal selection did not succeed. The findings were similar for companies who selected successful external candidates—their candidate pools contained more internal candidates than those of companies who selected an unsuccessful external candidate. If there is no clear reason to prefer external or internal candidates, then it pays to have a well-balanced pool of candidates so that the best one can be selected regardless of whether he or she is internal or external.

We do not have a definitive answer about why this kind of variety is important. But we suspect that including a variety of highly qualified candidates in the candidate pool serves to make selectors more aware both of their selection criteria and of their comparison methods.

How to Recruit More Effectively

To recruit more effectively, you need to ask yourself some questions. You also need to think about the questions that potential applicants will be asking themselves. Here are a few guidelines.

Selection committee members need to ask themselves questions like these:

- Have we included both good information about ourselves and realistic expectations in our materials so that we can give candidates a realistic job preview? Did we use the information that we gathered on organizational needs, position, and candidate requirements?
- Are we being realistic about our candidate requirements so that there is a viable pool of candidates?
- What is our bench strength? And who is next in the succession plan? Is that person ready?
- Do we already have executives who have the needed expertise for our organizational needs and position requirements?
- Do we want or need to look at outside candidates? Is there a particular candidate we would like to recruit?

- Have we asked knowledgeable insiders and outsiders for rec-ommendations for candidates? Have we put advertisements in useful locations? Have we done our own research or hired a search firm to find candidates for us?
- Should we consider other candidates we have been impressed with?
- Are there any consultants we have worked with and know well who might be a fit for this job?
- Have we considered all sources? Have we properly tapped into a variety of different populations?
- Do we have enough candidates to make a good selection? Have we cast our net wide enough to get the top-quality candidates yet narrow enough so that we aren't getting those who would not fit?
- Why would a smart, energetic, ambitious executive want to work for us rather than going somewhere else?

At the same time, the candidates who are viewing your organi-zation will also be asking themselves questions. Here are some of those:

- Do I want this job?
- Is this a prestigious or attractive organization? With good financials? And not likely to be taken over in the foreseeable future?
- Is this a stable job or one I would use as a stepping-stone into another position?
- Will this mean moving? Do I or my family want to move? Is the organization supportive in helping us move?
- What are the pay, the benefits, the fringe benefits?
- Is this team made up of top-quality individuals with whom I would like to work?
- Is it worth the bother to jump into the pool?

- Am I getting a real picture of the organization and the position? Or am I going to be shocked when I get their real expectations once on the job?
- What's in it for me?
- Do my values fit with this organization?
- Does my style of working fit with the culture?
- Will I be working in a supportive climate with people whom I will respect or enjoy?
- Who will help me learn to fit into this new culture?
- Will there be ongoing support from the organization to help me succeed? Are the criteria for success clear?
- Will I be able to make a positive contribution?
- Are there hidden agendas that I need to be careful about?
- What is my sense about how the other executives are treated and how they feel about the company?

Summary

There is a war going on at the top of today's organizations, a battle for talent (Chambers et al., 1998). Companies are suffering from a shortage of qualified top executives. To help resolve this situation, they need to consider seriously this step in the selection process. High-quality candidates are crucial to a successful selection process. In this chapter we discussed how to attract quality talent. Organizations need to give an appealing yet realistic image of themselves to possible candidates—including information from their organizational needs assessment, position requirements, and candidate requirements. They need to treat all contacts with respect and they need to network continuously, even when they have no position openings.

We suggested five options for searching for quality talent: succession plans, nominations from knowledgeable others, advertising, research, and search firms. We also suggested ensuring that there is variety in the candidate pool. Today's candidate pools continue to be similar to those of the past—limited in race, gender, and age. However, we found evidence to suggest that including variety in the candidate pool may prompt a selection committee to be more aware of its selection criteria and comparison methods.

In the next chapter we address the heart of the selection process: making the selection decision, including using selection tools to gather information on candidates, gathering and using information from the candidates that matches organizational needs, position requirements, and candidate requirements, and the importance of using both rational and intuitive processes to make the actual decision.

Chapter Six

Making the Selection Decision

At this point you know what you are looking for, you have the right people to make the decision, and you have a qualified pool of candidates. Now is the time to start comparing the candidates in your pool against your organization, job, and candidate requirements and to get the best information about the candidates so that you can make an effective choice. This is the heart of the selection process: gathering and using information about the candidates. If you have done a good job up to this point, this step in the process will be relatively painless. But experience tells us that you are probably anxious and confused.

We have divided this chapter into three sections. The first section discusses the general tools used for gathering information on candidates. The second and third sections outline what really makes a difference: the kind of information sought and used during the matching process, and the way the decision is made.

Selection Tools

At the senior level, the matching process appears to be more subjective than at the lower levels. In a 1993 Center for Creative Leadership technical report, David DeVries lamented that corporate executives do not use more objective personnel selection tools. He continued, "In fact, those people who select senior executives have basically ignored the decades of research on personnel selection" (p. 17). Instead, he found, they rely on such selection tools as the interview, which is one of the least reliable techniques available unless you are a very skilled interviewer. Interestingly, even psychologists who conduct individual assessment of managerial candidates for corporate clients are likely to use subjective judgments although they do report a greater likelihood of considering scores on ability tests and personality tests in their judgments (Ryan & Sackett, 1987).

Our findings were the same. Both those who hire successfully and those who hire unsuccessfully continue to rely heavily on interviews, résumés, and references. (See Table 6.1.) Why do executives continue to rely on such tools when there have been many advances in other processes in the selection arena? There are several reasons for this state of affairs.

First, executives have considerable faith in their own personal judgment. They believe they are uniquely capable of in-depth assessments of candidates through thorough interviews. They are used to making a lot of tough decisions without sufficient information. Because of their track record, they are "right" more often than not. They are used to having their judgments carried out unquestioned. We call this *minimal self-doubt*, and it seems to be a necessary requirement for senior executives. Yet selection decisions are very complex. Executives may not be aware of the unconscious processes that can control their selection choices.

Second, these tools are simple to use and have face validity. Convincing and then scheduling candidates to participate in more intensive evaluations, such as an in-depth individual assessment (usually undertaken by a psychologist), is difficult and expensive.

Third, interviews, references, and résumés have little impact and intrude very little on the candidates' lives. People dislike being judged, appraised, rank-ordered, and evaluated. Placing high-level executives in "assessment fishbowls" to be observed for high-stakes positions is threatening. Those seeking to hire an executive do not want to alienate potential candidates with methods that may infringe on their privacy. Many executives in our interview study

Table 6.1 Tools Used in the Executive Selection Process.

Tools	Percentage of Executives Mentioning
Interviews	87
Résumés	73
References	69
Peer reviews	52
Executive search firms	37
Tests and other instruments	36
Performance appraisals	36
Subordinate reviews	24
Succession plans	18
Assessment centers	8
Individual assessments	2

Note: N = 317
Source: Sessa, Kaiser, Taylor, & Campbell, 1998.

shared the concern of one of them, who said, "No psychological testing was done because of fear of lawsuits."

Thus, rarely used are succession plans, assessment centers, and individual assessments. When given the opportunity to use professional assessments and other sophisticated tools, executives found them to be very helpful. Still, we found that even when using more sophisticated tools such as assessments or performance appraisals, no one tool alone created a significant advantage. Unfortunately, there is no "silver bullet" when it comes to selection. No one tool guarantees success. Instead, what seems to matter is collecting the information about the candidate that specifically matches what the organization needs. Thus, search tools need to vary depending on the kind of information that is necessary to assess the candidates.

Organizations tend to vary their selection tools to collect information on internal and external candidates. For external candidates, they turn to search firms. For internal candidates, they use performance appraisals, succession plans, and subordinate reviews. But it is actually better to use the *same* tools to gather the same information on all candidates—making sure that the tools are chosen based on the kind of information that is being sought.

Seeking and Using Balanced Information

Thus, what is important is a disciplined gathering of balanced information that taps into the required hard-side and soft-side skills needed from the candidates. Then, carefully use that specific information to make the decision whether each particular potential candidate will or will not fit the specifications outlined.

Too often, executives gather information that does not measure what they have said they need. Selectors look for far fewer qualifications than were mentioned. This is not a rare phenomenon—even placement professionals in lower levels of the organization often rely heavily on only two attributes to make their decisions (Gardner, Kozloski, & Hults, 1991).

In our interviews we found that both those who hired a candidate who was ultimately successful and those who hired a candidate who was unsuccessful sought and used information on each candidate's hard-side requirements, such as expertise, track record, business and job experience, skills and knowledge, and academic background. They also looked for such soft-side skills as interpersonal skills and leadership abilities. However, those who made a successful hire went further: they also sought and used information on personal characteristics, values, and fit with the superior and the organization.

The importance of considering both hard-side and soft-side attributes was further supported in our simulation study. Teams that paid attention to both sets of skills were more likely to choose the correct candidate than teams that concentrated on one set or the other. The choice of Michael Armstrong as CEO at AT&T appears to reflect a balanced process. With a background at IBM's communications team and experience as chairman of Hughes Electronics,

Armstrong understood the technology world, and his quick grasp of information and decisiveness allowed him to move quickly.

Balancing Hard-Side and Soft-Side Skills

One of the successful selectors in our interview study told us, "The track record is the most important factor. It's much better to have continuous success, even if smaller than one big success." In other words, an executive needs to have the technical skills necessary to do the job.

However, at the senior executive level, hard-side skills by themselves are not sufficient. Earle Mauldin of BellSouth told us, "In order to enter a corporation, one needs to evidence a level of technical skills and experience. In order to move up into a position, one needs to have people skills, emphasize empowerment, and be a good communicator."

Executives must have skills in this area to be successful. For example, the more than three hundred senior executives in General Motors and Delphi Automotives were asked to rank twenty-one executive skills in importance. The executives of both companies rated *seasoned judgment, shaping strategy,* and *inspiring trust* as three of the four most important leadership skills; all three are soft-side skills. But unfortunately, many executive candidates who are fully qualified when it comes to their hard-side skills are lacking in soft-side skills. One executive told us, "About 95 percent of the people had the economic credentials and expertise, but they did not necessarily have the ability to interact as part of a team."

Those who hire an executive who is successful are likely to say something like the following, "The individual was chosen on the basis of interpersonal criteria. He seemed to have energy, and to share a similar communication style and general chemistry with the president." Those who hire unsuccessful executives lament, "In hindsight, we should have emphasized communication and interpersonal skills more." They also say, "We did not completely and properly assess this candidate's ability to move outside of the strictly technical area and into the area of leadership, which implied having a vision for the company, seeing the big picture, and finally making tough decisions to put the vision of the corporation into operation."

Judging Fit

The concept of fit is ambiguous, yet critical. During the selection process the search committee uses available information to create an ideal candidate. When selectors consider candidates, they do so one at a time by developing a composite picture for each separate candidate. Each candidate is usually designated as having a distinctive quality that separates him or her from the others. For example, executives might refer to two candidates in the following manner: "Pat is our marketing candidate. Carl is a turnaround artist." Each candidate with accompanying sobriquet is then compared with the ideal candidate to determine amount of fit. However, defining fit is problematic under these circumstances. We recommend therefore that the selection committee carefully detail what it means by fit. What makes a good fit is too often measured by the committee's comfort level with a particular candidate. But fit also needs to refer to organizational needs, job requirements, and candidate requirements. Sears, Roebuck and Company provides an interesting historical example of an attempt to define fit. At one time, the top-level executives operationalized fit in terms of height. Apparently, an early CEO at the firm believed that standing six feet two inches or taller was important for effectiveness (Katz, 1987).

Unless an organization is clear about what is meant by fit, it may not be able to support a new hire in areas where he or she does not fit but where success is necessary to accomplish the overall job. For example, one company was looking for a vice president of marketing where it had previously had little marketing expertise. Clearly, marketing talent was needed. However, to get the rest of the staff to listen to someone with a marketing perspective required a cultural shift in how they felt about marketing information. For the new VP to succeed, the CEO was going to have to support clearly a different kind of decision making that did not seem to fit with the culture.

Thus, there can be conflicts between what is a fit with the culture and what is a fit with emerging strategy. If the senior executives are not clear about this tension, they will not be able to support the new executive and will not get the organizational results they are hiring for. In the preceding example, the new marketing VP who was selected ultimately chose to leave the organization.

Making the Selection Decision

Good executives know how to make decisions using a logical, rational approach. First, they state and define the problem; second, they make explicit the goals and alternatives; third, they consider the situation and the consequences of each of the different alternatives; fourth, they evaluate each of the consequences; and fifth, they make the correct decision. Right?

The Importance of Intuition

Surprisingly, this is not the approach we heard in descriptions of successful selections. Top-level executives said they rely on intuition or "gut feel" during selections of other executives. Furthermore, those who hired a successful executive were more likely to use intuition than those who hired an unsuccessful executive. One executive who hired a successful executive described it as a "fairly intuitive process of adding information up, putting it all in the hopper, then putting it together." Similarly, teams who make successful selections often begin by advocating candidates and letting intuition and instinct dominate the very beginning of their conversation. When teams do this, we found they were more likely to succeed in using a rational process later in their decision.

Balancing Rationality and Intuition

The rational decision-making model that students learn in a business class does not take into account two things. First, the rational decision-making model tells us how to make the decision *correctly*. But it does not tell us how to make the *correct* decision. The difference is important.

Second, the rational model does not take into account the role of cumulative expertise and experience—that is, what we call intuition. Intuition is based on extensive experience in problem analysis, problem solving, and implementation. Intuition is the most advanced stage of knowing (Melone, 1994). As a form of well-honed expertise, intuition allows executives to increase speed and accuracy in selection to the point that they often lose sight of exactly how they make the decision in the first place. Often the terms *gut feel* and *intuition* have a concrete basis and should not be ignored.

One senior executive reflected on his own use of intuition in the hiring process. He said, "While we pay a lot of attention to the candidate's credentials, if we don't get the right gut feel, we won't go with the candidate." He went on to add, "My intuition has gotten more trustworthy as I become more experienced. Early in my career I made some intuitive calls that turned out fine, and some that turned out lousy. Intuition really has a lot to do with experience and maturity."

In another example, in one team we observed during our executive selection simulation, a highly intuitive executive had selected the best choice whereas others had ranked this choice third or fourth out of four. In the discussion, the executive kept saying he thought the candidate was clearly the best but he couldn't explain why. The rest of the team wanted data to support that position, and he couldn't provide it. Frustrated by this executive's inability to explain his position, the team ended up not adopting his choice but chose instead another candidate who was not as well qualified.

For novices who are not familiar with a situation, may not know what key features in the situation to focus on, and do not have a repertoire of what has worked and what has not worked in the past, it is helpful, and perhaps even necessary, to follow the rational decision model to increase the likelihood of making a "correct" decision.

In contrast, when experts make decisions, although they too may use a conscious and deliberate approach, they are able to take bigger steps at a time because they can draw on their experience. They have already been in similar situations. They more quickly focus on key features. They search through memories and accumulated knowledge. In this way, experts can quickly discount some potential candidates as not being a good fit in this situation, or as not working, or as having had a negative impact in similar situations that they have encountered before. This cumulative experience allows them to more quickly come to a conclusion. Thus a great deal of what novices must make explicit, experts can do implicitly. They arrive at their solution, why they think it is correct, and why they think other options are incorrect or not as good without knowing how they do so. Our executives told us, "Intuition and gut feeling are important to selection. But I have a hard time articulating the process." They said, "What I rely on most is my intuition. Every time I've ignored my intuitive reactions I have regretted it."

Advantages and Disadvantages of Trusting Intuition

Selecting a candidate is a very complex decision. Successful executives who have a great range of experience have turned a rational and laborious decision-making process into an intuitive process that they can draw on quickly but can't always explain. The important factor is that they are taking into account strategic issues, negotiation, politics, and socioemotional issues simultaneously.

For example, one executive who had hired an unsuccessful executive told us, "I felt the candidate who was selected was not entirely honest in the interview, the references were not accurate concerning his abilities, and performance reviews were actually measuring traits other than those needed in this particular position." In hindsight, to the detriment of this selection process, this executive realized that he had not heeded his own intuition.

However, intuition that cannot be substantiated can become a weakness. Again, high-level executives are accustomed to being expert decision makers and are not used to being challenged. They often must make decisions based on information they have readily available and use their intuition to fill in the gaps. They can at times become inflexible when presented with new perspectives and information. For example, one executive stated that he tended to have a bias in his selection criteria. He said, "I tend to see all situations as fires because *I am a good firefighter.* I frame everything in terms of fires instead of being more objective. Sometimes I analyze the situation incorrectly, and then when I rely on my gut I am picking for the wrong skills—that is, fighting fires."

In our simulation, most of the executives assertively advocated for their choice rather than openly soliciting information from other team members. We found this behavior to be acceptable at the beginning of the conversation, but remaining inflexible throughout the process is detrimental.

When executives become invested in being right and saving face, they are even less likely to challenge their intuitive assumptions. When the possibility of guilt, anxiety, embarrassment, or a chance to look really good are added into the intuition equation, the executive often becomes unable to differentiate the factual and intuitive from the emotional and intuitive.

When the decision is being made about other people, the problem is further compounded for top-level executives. As we indicated in Chapter One, many of the top-level executives we interviewed are not experts at selection. Twenty percent of those we spoke with had never been involved in the selection of another top-level executive. Those who had had participated in an average of six selections. Relying on intuition when you have little expertise puts you at risk of being unable to distinguish facts from stereotypes or emotions. Relying on intuition when you have little expertise in selection tends to result in a crude, back-of-the-envelope, emotional decision. This isn't surprising. We all bring with us past experiences dating back to our early childhood to make sense of and understand new experiences. Our initial judgments of people by necessity are colored by our past experiences, and they do not always correspond with what these people are actually like.

The bottom line is that intuition is not fail-safe. Attachment to the decision, time pressure, lack of facts, impulsivity, stress, fatigue, and confusion can all interfere. Thus, it is best not to rely on intuition alone but rather to see it as one more piece of information to consider. If your "gut" does not agree with the "rational" decision, it is worth taking the time to figure out why. We found that in successful teams, executives first advocated for particular candidates, then gathered information in a disciplined way, remaining open to additional information. Thus, they used both data and intuition to guide their decision.

Steps in the Decision-Making Process

Here are some guidelines to follow in the decision-making process.

Take a Disciplined Approach. Make sure you are gathering information that matches the organizational assessment and the position and candidate requirements. Proceeding rationally is an effective way to make decisions (Dean & Sharfman, 1996).

Fit the selection tools to the information you want to obtain. To assess hard-side attributes, get information from the interview, references, résumés, and 360-degree assessments. Also, tailor questions to the specific skills you are trying to assess. For example, if one of the candidate requirements is for an individual who can turn around a failing division in the company, candidates and their references should be asked to describe specific situations, actions, and results relating to their experience with turnarounds.

It is important not to rely on the interview to assess soft-side skills, because interviews can only assess these superficially. Instead, use psychological assessments, subordinate and customer feedback, and 360-degree feedback that is geared toward the specific soft-side skills that need to be assessed. For example, if the person you seek is someone who can inspire trust, talk to the candidate's subordinates and customers. We've never heard a candidate admit to being untrustworthy!

Treat all candidates similarly (especially if some are internal and some are external), and make sure you get similar information on each. It is difficult enough to compare candidates with the picture of the ideal candidate that was created through the organizational assessment, job requirements, and candidate requirements and with each of the other candidates when you have the same information on each. Doing so when you have a different set of information on each candidate is nearly impossible.

Check Your Intuition. If you are satisfied that you have done a good job spelling out the organizational needs and the requirements for both the position and the candidate and that you have actually gained that information from each of the candidates, *and* if your intuition has been useful in the past, then by all means use your intuition to help make the final decision. To the extent that your expertise is based on logical and well-founded experience, then so is your intuition. Still, when you find yourself relying on intuition, you may want to ask yourself the following questions to make sure that you have used all other possible sources of information as well:

- Have we asked other people for information or what their impressions are? Are we including this information or discounting it?

- Have our initial impressions of this candidate changed as we have gotten to know him or her?

- What did we learn new about the person as we talked to references and shared our own perceptions?

- What kinds of judgments are we making that are inferences that we have not backed up with hard data or asked about directly?
- Does this person make any of us uncomfortable, and why?
- How different is this person from the rest of the team—are those differences what we are looking for?
- Can we find data to challenge our intuition, not just to reinforce it?

Summary

This chapter examined the heart of the selection process—making the decision to select a candidate. It discussed the importance of choosing selection tools that fit the information that the selectors need from the candidates. No perfect selection tool will automatically identify the best candidate. Today's executives rely heavily on interviews, references, and résumés—all of which may be good for gathering some types of information but are not necessarily the best or only choices for all situations. What is crucial is getting and using the information that is needed based on the organizational needs, job requirements, and candidate requirements—not based on the selection tool used. Once good, balanced information on each candidate (including hard-side skills, soft-side skills, and fit) is obtained, the selection committee will be ready to make the decision by using both rational and intuitive processes.

As the next chapter shows, once the selection has been made and the candidate has agreed to accept the position, your job is not yet over. Both the new hire and the organization need to be prepared—especially if the new hire will be working in a position that requires him or her to change the organization in some way. New hires need to be integrated, supported, and continuously developed, with the understanding that it may take up to eighteen months for them to master the new position.

Chapter Seven

Integrating the New Executive

Helmut Schmidt, the former chancellor of West Germany, was once asked if he thought leaders can be developed or if leadership is an inherent capability that we simply need to learn to recognize and groom. He answered, "First it takes two people, then it takes nine months, then it takes fifty years." The implication was that there must be some innate ability, but the person needs experience in order to fulfill that ability.

Even the most senior executive does not appear on the first day ready to jump into a new job. Once you have selected the most appropriate candidate, your real work is just beginning. New executives must learn a demanding new job, develop new or different relationships with key people, deal with unspoken organizational norms, and perhaps operate in an alien culture. Moreover, their actions in the first few months of the job create long-term perceptions about how effective they are going to be.

The role that the new hire's superior and the selection committee play in helping that individual fit in with the organization, the job, and new peers is crucial to him or her. No matter how good the selection process and how perfect the match between the organization and the executive, the likelihood of failure is much higher unless that individual is properly integrated into the position and the organization. This is true for both executives who are promoted from within the organization and those who are hired from the outside. Even experienced insiders go through a resocialization period when they change positions.

In our interview study, less than one-third of newly hired executives received any sort of integration or development for their new position. Less than one-fourth received support from their superiors. Very few received any support at all from other executives, including peers, subordinates, or customers.

Furthermore, this situation was true across the board. We found that those executives brought in from the outside were no more likely to receive any sort of introduction into the organization than those promoted from within. In addition, even though one-fourth of our selectors mentioned that the position was seen as a developmental one for the internal new hires, they received little support on entry into their new position. It was as if the promotion itself resulted in a developmental outcome.

The Link Between Selection and Development

Very few of the selectors we interviewed acknowledged that executive development and executive selection should be integrated. Yet, as McCall, Lombardo, and Morrison (1988) found, developmental experiences are key to the eventual success or failure of an executive. So why is there such a disconnect between selection and development? The reason may have to do with the debate about whether executives occur by nature (they are born with the skills, abilities, and characteristics necessary for running an organization) or by nurture (any person can be developed to have the necessary knowledge, skills, abilities, and characteristics necessary for running an organization).

We believe that the "nature-nurture" dichotomy has set up a false belief in the minds of many executives. We need to stop perpetuating the notion that selection and development are wholly different processes. An executive who is selected *must* be developed. And an executive who is selected has probably *already received* a great deal of development, whether through on-the-job or off-the-job experiences. Selection and development go hand in hand.

In this chapter, we will talk about the kinds of support that are necessary once a new executive accepts a job offer. Integration, preparatory support, and development affect whether the new hire will ultimately be successful or unsuccessful in the position. Those who are successful are more likely to have benefited from such efforts than those who are unsuccessful. For example, one of the executives we interviewed said about an unsuccessful selection, "Part of the lack of success is not just that the selection process was inappropriate, but rather that oftentimes once a person is hired we take very much a 'sink-or-swim' approach to the new executive. We don't provide a lot of training and development once the person is hired." In contrast, another executive told us that a new hire had succeeded because of "tremendous support from the boss, and in this particular case, the boss had actually done this business development job for two and one-half years and so was able to provide support, encouragement, and freedom to the executive, and to utilize a more long-term emphasis in the evaluation process." At Rank Xerox, researchers found that what happened in the first few months on the job—particularly when it came to assistance from a formal or informal mentor—had an impact on an employee's attitude toward the organization (Mabey & Iles, 1991).

This integration step of the selection process is necessary for two reasons. First, it prepares the new executive for what to expect from the organization. Second, but just as important, it prepares the organization for what to expect from the individual. This period of adaptation is crucial for both parties. The situation can be likened to what occurs with an organ transplant—the new organ is necessary for the vital functioning of the organism, yet the body's natural reaction is to defend itself against anything new and unusual. The corporate tendency toward rejection, although always present, is intensified if an executive has been selected purposely to change elements of the culture. As one executive whose new hire was ultimately unsuccessful lamented, "Nothing was done to prepare the person or the organization for the transplant. No training was given to the candidate regarding his position."

Preparing the Individual

According to a number of organizational experts (for example, Gabarro, 1987, 1988; Nicholson & West, 1989), it can take a top-level executive up to eighteen months to master a new position. Newly hired executives do not hit the ground running on their first day. This eighteen-month period can be divided into two phases. First come early integration and assimilation, next come development and learning so that the executive can continue to master the job.

The First Phase: Early Assimilation

The first stage is one of great anxiety and transition for newly hired executives, and it begins earlier than you may think. What happens from the moment executives enter a selection process (that is, before accepting the position) has a lasting impact on their behaviors and attitudes and how they are seen by others.

Integration and assimilation have three related purposes: *to inform* new executives about what they are expected to do and how they are expected to work, *to transmit the culture*, and *to teach* the new executive the politics and power dynamics of the organization. Mentoring newly hired executives to help them learn this information rapidly is critical because this information is typically unseen, not easily recognized, and unspoken.

Informing. It is crucial that the step of learning the ropes is tied to the organizational needs and job requirements. Communicating this information to new hires along with a plan explaining how they will be assessed helps make the assimilation process go more smoothly.

Although organizational experts say that it can take eighteen months to assimilate fully to the job, the reality is that if executives do not hit the ground running in the first six months, they will be labeled as failures. Executives are *not* given much time to learn the ropes of a new position or a new organization. When it comes to performance, we found that executives are evaluated on how they perform on the job immediately. They are given six months before being held accountable for organizational results. As for relationships, external hires are given a six-month grace period to build relationships with others, but internal hires are evaluated immediately on their relationships. This is problematic because internal hires may also have some delicate relationships to manage.

Transmitting the Culture. Understanding organizational culture is one of the most powerful determinants of succeeding in an organization. But culture is not apparent to the naked eye, and it is particularly difficult for newcomers to decipher. All executives bring with them an accumulation of attitudes and values that have been shaped by previous work cultures and experiences. The more senior the position they enter, the more they may expect to be able to shape the new culture. This normal attitude of urgency and assumed impact can cause problems.

Misjudging the culture can put a new executive in a real bind. As we stated in the preceding section, new executives are under immediate pressure to perform. Their success depends on their ability to affect the organization quickly. Yet if they stumble unaware across important organizational norms, they may unintentionally mobilize powerful resistance against their actions. For example, in one company, a very talented new chief information officer began quietly telling a plant manager how much he was going to help him and all the changes he was going to make. The plant manager responded in a confrontational way, saying, "I'm not making any changes until you prove to me your ideas will work." The new CIO had violated an important norm in this company—not telling independent "old-timers" how to do their jobs. He had to build relationships, trust, and credibility first, no matter how urgent he thought his task was.

One company president told us, "Our new VP is very competent but he is not going to survive. When he had been on the job only two weeks, he went behind a peer's back to the CEO to make sure he got his way. We don't do that in this company. His peer is just biding his time; eventually he will get him."

This relationship-versus-task dilemma is one of the easiest norms to violate. In one organization in which relationships were held high in importance, a new executive collected information from a variety of different teams as part of an assessment about the effectiveness of a particular issue facing the organization (which she was hired to deal with). She then shared that information, some of it critical of other teams, with the CEO without discussing her observations with the teams in question. Although the information she had gotten was correct, her ability to use that information was hindered because the teams felt that her method of doing so had violated them and they refused to work with her. Fortunately, in this case, intense coaching helped her save her career and reestablish relationships with the other teams.

New executives need to be instructed in the new culture and add new or different attitudes and values to their current repertoire. They need to be given the information to help them fit into the organization—to know what is sacred and what is changeable.

Explaining Politics and Power Dynamics. Much of the work of executives centers around their ability to influence. It is critical for them to learn quickly how decisions really get made and who the influencers are. Thus, it is imperative for them to form key relationships and gain acceptance while they learn their new roles. As we saw in Chapter Two, a positive working relationship between the executive and subordinates is one of the factors that predicts whether that executive will be successful. From the beginning, successful relationships provide executives with social support, lead to acceptance into the organization, help transmit the culture, and give them the organizational know-how to understand "how things really get done around here." As one executive who made a successful hire confided, "If I hadn't provided coaching for this person on his interpersonal skills, he probably would not have succeeded."

The Second Phase: Continued Development

After the executive has been in the position for six months, early assimilation evolves into continued development and job mastery. At this stage it becomes even more apparent that selection and development are inseparable pieces in the process of creating talent and leadership at the top of today's organizations. Even the best experts need to learn continually in order to remain successful in a position.

This is not a new phenomenon. In a 1933 report to stockholders, H. S. Richardson, CEO of Richardson Vicks, said, "From a corporate standpoint, the danger is that managers gradually and insensibly lose the ability to recognize and adjust to new and challenging business conditions."

Organizations change, jobs change, coworkers change, individual executives change. The position the executive is hired for evolves over the period of time he or she holds the job. What works well in one situation becomes a weakness in the next. Therefore, an executive must continue to develop on the job. Astute executives bring the concepts of selection and development together by linking both to the organization's strategy. They see selection not just as an initial hiring decision but as selections for key assignments, task forces, projects, and work relationships (Hall, 1995).

The Center for Creative Leadership has a rich history in exploring how executives develop on the job. We use that experience to help identify the most important areas in which to coach an executive. Obviously, any new job involves transitions, with a change in work role, job content, and responsibility. If executives are to master these transitions, they need to find new ways of thinking about and responding to problems and opportunities. Executives must "prove themselves" all over again.

Central to mastering transitions is the ability to understand other people's points of view. Learning that different skills are required for dealing with different people is an important part of the developmental process in a new job. This includes learning how to achieve cooperation among people over whom the executive does not have direct authority, such as clients, peers, joint-venture partners, project teams, task forces, and top management teams.

Perhaps the most significant developmental skill that executives can possess is the ability to self-monitor and understand their impact on other people and situations. (Like the ability to maintain good relationships, which we mention throughout this book, self-monitoring and understanding one's impact on others are components of *emotional intelligence*.) The ability to self-monitor implies both a self-awareness about one's impact and the ability to make changes based on that effectiveness. Coaching executives about their impact and helping them learn how to assess themselves realistically can be one of the most valuable things you can do to help a newly hired executive succeed. The more an executive is self-aware, the more he or she is able to develop continually and adapt to new situations. In one study of a Fortune 100 company that compared high- and low-performing executives, the high-performing executives rarely overestimated their abilities—that is, they were able to self-monitor. Lower-performing executives consistently overrated their leadership abilities; they were doing a poor job of assessing their impact in comparison with how others were assessing them.

It is important to be clear about the skills that are necessary for the success of a new executive and to communicate them to the executive. In our work with key executives we are continually surprised at how often the executive and his or her boss disagree on the different leadership skills essential for the success of that executive. More important, neither the superiors nor the new executives are aware that they have differences! The clearer the boss is about his or her expectations, the greater the chance that the boss, the newly hired executive, and the organization will be focusing on the same things to get the best results.

Preparing the Organization

One of our executives who had hired an unsuccessful executive told us, "The organization was not ready to assimilate this type of person into the company culture. Things were done to prepare the person, but nothing was done to prepare the organization." An organization must be prepared to accept the new executive. The behaviors and messages from the executive team about what they expect from the new executive and what they are looking for are critical. This kind of preparation is especially true if the executive is brought in from the outside and is expected to make some sort of change in the organization.

When executives (ambitious people, with impressive track records) are offered a position and then accept it, they make two assumptions. First, they assume that the people they met during the interview are those with whom they will be working closely. They may be shocked to find out that they will be working with a different set of folks with different personalities and different sets of expectations, people who have no idea what the search committee was looking for or why the particular candidate was hired and who may even disagree with the search committee entirely.

Second, newly hired executives assume that what was said during the interview process was true. This can be problematic—because part of the selection committee's job is to sell the candidate on the organization. Organizational problems or resistance may not have been adequately discussed with the executive. Because new executives are ambitious and know the importance of making their mark early, they already have ideas about how to act. They may be shocked to find out that the messages sent them were not totally agreed upon by all parties. Organizations rarely respond with one voice. There will definitely be some in the organization who really are not interested in changing.

To minimize these kinds of problems, the CEO and the search committee need to be explicit and clear in their communication about why this person was chosen. They should do this not just when they initially announce the choice but rather communicate continually who this person is, why he was chosen over others, what he is expected to do, how he is going to help the organization achieve its strategy, and how his success will be measured.

When people with whom the new executive will be working have been included on the selection committee, they will have a clear and realistic idea about what is needed in the position. They cannot only communicate it realistically to the candidates but also aid in communicating the expectations to the rest of the organization. Importantly, senior executives need to look for public opportunities to support the new executive.

When the New Executive Is Expected to Be a Change Agent

The importance of preparing the organization for the executive is especially great when the newly hired executive is expected to bring about change. Unfortunately, we have seen too many examples of a CEO hiring a new executive—usually an external one—specifically to be a change agent and then, when the inevitable tensions about changes arise, the CEO backing down, leaving the new executive unsupported. This is an impossible situation to succeed in. Katy Barclay, vice president for global human resources at General Motors, has thought this through clearly. She says, "When a company is hiring a change agent they need to be very clear about what they are trying to change and declare openly that they are looking for change. That way the organization lays down a path for the new person to walk down. They must be clear with the newly hired person about what the obstacles are and how big they are."

One Fortune 50 company deliberately chose as one of their vice presidents an executive whose culture was very different from their own. The man was aggressive, forceful, a no-nonsense sort of leader—his style very different from the bureaucratic culture he was brought in to change. The dramatic actions he took, which included eliminating several thousand jobs, were met with skepticism and predictions of failure. But when the CEO then promoted this executive to president, he sent a message to the entire organization that he was serious about change.

If you have brought someone in specifically because he or she is different from the current culture, you may find that even you, yourself are uncomfortable. If this is the case, it is important for you to know that everything that you say and do will be interpreted by the organization as either a supportive or unsupportive act.

Integrating the Individual

As part of the integration process, it can be useful to help the new executive understand the history of the organization (culture derives from history), introduce him or her to the leadership of the organization, and tell him or her what other successful executives have done.

For example, shortly after accepting a position, new executives at KPMG (Kymveld Peat Marwick Goerdeler)—one of the "Big Six" professional services firms—receive attractively designed organizational materials and are contacted by those individuals who will provide a core of support through the assimilation process. Much emphasis is put on the executive's first day, but the assimilation continues beyond that day. During the acclimation period, the organization outlines its expectations and offers an on-site training program that conveys the company history, strategy, policy, and benefits and acquaints the new executive with company leaders. Later, there is an additional period in which the new executive learns the market, customers, and business plans. Finally, when the new hire reaches the status of established employee, he or she receives progress reviews, updates, and performance assessments (Winkler & Janger, 1998).

Texas Instruments is another good example of a company that knows how to integrate new executives. The process at TI begins during the recruitment stages. The potential hire's peers, subordinates, and supervisors all participate. As we explained in more detail in Chapter Five, including such a group leads to better selection decisions. But TI finds that this also helps to begin the actual transition process because the prospective executive gets to know a lot about the company, its people, and the job during the selection process (Winkler & Janger, 1998).

Selecting new executives is an expensive and time-consuming process. Taking the time to help them learn the ropes, the culture, and company politics is a small additional price to pay to ensure their success. Early and timely feedback on how they are doing is especially helpful. Setting up realistic time frames for achievement of goals and agreeing on evaluation measures help the executive master the job more quickly and avoid costly mistakes.

It is very useful to help new executives create feedback loops. Their learning curve will initially be very steep. They will be overwhelmed with the complexity of the task. Helping them create systems to monitor how they are progressing through the transition and the effectiveness of their new relationships provides them with sound information to learn from. Taking the time to discuss the important leadership criteria can help them focus on the most important of the myriad demands they are confronting.

What the New Executive Can Do

Although the organization's role is very important, newly hired executives should not wait for the organization to take the lead in their socialization and development. There is a lot they can do on their own to prepare themselves for the transition. An executive speaking about a successful executive he had hired noted, "Six weeks prior to his arrival to the organization, he started to develop an internal knowledge of the relationships with the people in the company. Later when he came to the company, he took the initiative to introduce himself to people at all levels."

In contrast, one of the executives we interviewed told us about an individual who was not successful. When he showed up "for his first day on the job, his appearance had changed from being properly attired in business suits to wearing jeans and boots." In another case, members of a business team reflected on why their new vice president had lasted only one year and told us, "When she showed up it was quite a shock to us. We felt that our team set the standard for appearing credible and businesslike, and our new vice president showed up on the first day of work wearing a casual pantsuit and inviting people to go on a hike with her that weekend. She brought a lot of innovation to the company, but we were not ready for those changes that fast."

If the organization does not take the first step toward good integration, new hires should be proactive. They need to learn everything they can about the organization, its history, and critical business transactions. They need to introduce themselves to others and interview them about what makes people successful in this organization. They need to find out what other employees' key business issues are, what excites them, what worries them, and what they are looking for from leadership. New executives need to ask key executives what they would like them to accomplish in the new position. They can also learn about fatal mistakes that other executives have made.

Furthermore, new hires need to understand that what they heard in the selection process is probably not quite reality on the job. They need to be realistic and prepared. They need to work actively to find out what the potential pitfalls are. They can get help in understanding how much tension the organization can tolerate. They can talk with their superiors to learn about how they will be evaluated and what will be considered important in the evaluation. They can get their superiors' and peers' help in setting up feedback loops. They can pay specific attention to relationship-building and assess how well they are doing in this area themselves. They must balance the need to make their mark with the need to learn about their job, the organization, the culture, and the people.

Summary

In this chapter, we discussed the importance of the continued development of the newly hired executive. The executives in our interview study indicated that rarely are newly hired executives given any support, integration, or development once they are in the position. However, the few new hires who did receive such assistance were likely to be successful—indicating that selection and development are inextricably linked.

Both the newly hired executive and the organization need to work at assimilation. The organization needs to ensure that the new executive learns the ropes, the culture, the company politics and power dynamics, and then continues to be developed on the job. The organization also needs to prepare itself for the new executive through continued communication about and public support of the executive.

This chapter is the final one in the description of our system for ensuring successful selection in an organization. As we have shown, use a team to make the selection decision. Then take a systematic approach that begins with assessment of the organization needs and position requirements in order to define the ideal candidate requirements. This list of candidate requirements will help you attract quality talent, decide what kind of information to collect from candidates, and make the final decision among candidates, and it will help the new hire assimilate and develop into the position.

In the next chapter, we discuss a related subject: the increasing popularity of hiring high-level executives from outside the organization as well as the increasing recognition that external executives hired at a high level are less likely to be successful than internal hires.

Chapter Eight

Internal Versus External Candidates

In Chapters Three through Seven we explained a team-based, systematic process that can be used to help improve selection decision making at the very top of organizations. This chapter addresses another specific issue that affects the selection process at the top: the growing practice of hiring external high-level executives.

The Paradox

The paradox is this: although top executives are increasingly looking outside their organizations for high-level executives when positions open, they are also struggling with the fact that external executives are less likely to succeed when hired.

External Hiring Is Increasing

Nearly one-third of the CEOs at the top of one thousand public companies are outsiders (Byrne, Reingold, & Melcher, 1997; Heller, 1997); in contrast, three decades ago only 9 percent were. Why is this so? Companies in rapidly changing industries are especially likely to look outside for a CEO. IBM presents a classic example. Around the time of the huge change in the computer business that came with the growth of the PC market, IBM's board of directors looked to outsider Lou Gerstner to turn the company around.

The same phenomenon is occurring one and two layers down from the CEO position. The executives we interviewed estimated that 41 percent of their hires are external. Although this number is slightly higher than estimates given elsewhere (for example, Byrne et al., 1997; Heller, 1997), reports of the trend of hiring high-level executives from outside the firm are consistent. We also found that when executives consider both internal candidates and external candidates during selection, they tend to select an external executive over the internal executives. Specifically, we found that selectors who say they specifically want to hire someone from within the organization do so 93 percent of the time, and those who say that they specifically want to bring someone new into the organization hire an external candidate 95 percent of the time. However, when selectors are open to considering both internal and external candidates, they choose an external candidate 75 percent of the time! This finding suggests that top-level executives may be biased toward external candidates and against internal candidates, at least during the selection process.

External Executives Are Less Likely to Be Seen as Successful

Yet once in the position, external hires are less likely to be seen as successful. We asked executives to estimate the failure rates of internal and external hires in their own organizations. They responded that their failure rate for internal hires was 24 percent whereas their failure rate for external hires was 35 percent! In addition, external executives were more than twice as likely to be fired after demonstrating poor performance as were internal hires (who were more likely to be demoted or otherwise moved aside because of poor performance).

A recent study that looked at executives moving into the position of president reported similar findings. Specifically, nearly two-thirds of new presidents hired from outside the organization left their companies within four years compared with only about one-third (38 percent) of those promoted from within (Ciampa & Watkins, 1999).

Thus, external executives seem to appear more favorable during the selection process, but once in the position they are less likely to be seen as successful. We believe that there are four related explanations for this paradox: organizations hire outsiders for different reasons than insiders; selection processes differ for internal and external candidates so that external executives appear more positive; once on the job, those hired from the outside are treated in the same way as internal hires but are evaluated differently; and finally, organizations hold different expectations for external executives than they do for internal executives.

Different Reasons for Hiring

Organizations choose internal and external candidates for different reasons. Not surprisingly, an internal executive is more likely to be selected for a position in order to provide him or her with a developmental challenge. When the company needs a new vision, it is also more likely to select an internal candidate. In contrast, when a company wants to introduce new technology, start a new business, and develop employees in general, selection committees more often turn to outside candidates.

Development

In our interviews, 34 percent of the selectors who chose an internal candidate stated that the executive was selected for developmental reasons. In contrast, 17 percent of those hiring from the outside said this. This finding suggests that selectors may view the position as a developmental experience for an internal candidate rather than try to find an executive whose experience best fits the position. GE and Citicorp are two notable companies that use high-level jobs as developmental experiences. At GE, an important factor in considering executive positions is to determine whose development will benefit most from the position. Similarly,

Citicorp tries to place executives in jobs for which they are no more than 60 to 70 percent prepared (Ohlott, 1998).

Vision

Twenty-four percent of those hiring internally stated that the position requirements included a need to create a new or different vision compared with 15 percent of those who chose an executive from outside. This finding is contrary to what we might expect to find based on the current thinking in the consulting world—that insiders lack the kind of perspective needed to change an organization. However, surely only an executive with a great deal of insight into an organization and its history, culture, and products can create a realistic and attainable vision for it.

New Technology

When an organization is dealing with updating or bringing in new technology, it is more likely to hire from outside. Seventeen percent of those ultimately hiring an external candidate stated that they were dealing with new technology versus 10 percent of those hiring an internal candidate. Executives believe that new technology means fundamental change for the organization. They look to the outside for someone who already has demonstrated knowledge and skills in technology rather than taking a chance on their own staff.

Start-Up

Only 12 percent of selectors who hired an internal candidate mentioned that their company had a start-up effort compared with 24 percent of those who hired an external candidate. They believed that it requires a fresh outside perspective, new skills, and different knowledge to successfully implement a new business in an already established structure.

Staff Development

Similarly, when executives perceive that their own workforce is in need of development, they are more likely to hire an external candidate to develop staff than hire someone internally. Fourteen percent of those who hired an external candidate stated that there was a need to develop people inside the organization compared with 6 percent of those who hired someone from the inside. Fresh from a different environment and new to this one, external executives are perceived to have the objectivity necessary to make developmental changes.

Both managing start-ups and developing staff deserve an additional mention here. Both of these conditions were described as especially challenging for the newcomer in Chapter Three. So although selectors show a marked preference for candidates from outside the organization when they are confronted with these situations, these hires are much less likely to succeed in the position than candidates hired from inside the organization.

Candidate Requirements

Organizations tend to choose internal candidates or external candidates depending on the particular candidate requirements needed. When organizations need someone who has company knowledge, product knowledge, and intelligence, they are more likely to select an insider. When they need an intensive background in a particular industry, a specific business experience, and managerial skills, they are more likely to select an outsider. (See Table 8.1.)

In Chapter Three we noted that when selectors talked about broad candidate requirements—such as managerial skills—they were less likely to choose a successful candidate. We suggested that the reason for this lack of success was the generality of the requirement; more specific and detailed understanding has to be reached regarding the meaning of "management skills."

Table 8.1 Candidate Requirements Mentioned: Internal Versus External Hires.

Candidate Requirements	Internal Executive Hired (Percentage)	External Executive Hired (Percentage)
Company knowledge	25	12
Product knowledge	10	4
Intelligence	21	12
Intensive experience in an industry	17	24
Specific business experience	12	27
Managerial skills	37	47

Note: N = 319; internal = 138; external = 181
Source: Sessa, Kaiser, Taylor, & Campbell, 1998.

Earlier we suggested that when top-level executives perceive their organization as being in a state of change (for example, because of start-up operations, use of new technology, or staff development), they believe that they need to bring in an executive with a specific background, experiences, and skills that are not available on staff. External executives are thus brought in to fill the need. In some cases it is evident that these external hires are unlikely to be successful. Unfortunately, the organizational situations in which external hires are favored are particularly challenging. It is difficult to determine if these executives are unsuccessful because they are external hires or because the jobs themselves are harder.

In contrast, when top-level executives perceive their organizations as being in a more stable state, they are more likely to see an open position as a developmental one and as one that needs an individual who is intimately familiar with the organization. In such cases, the internal hire faces an inherently easier task. The selectors are likely to have a discussion about how the position can stretch or develop employees.

These findings lead us to an interesting and important point. When selectors consider internal hires, their question often is, "What can this position offer this executive?" When selectors consider external hires, their question often is, "What can this executive offer this position?"

Different Selection Processes

In addition to having different reasons for hiring internal and external candidates, selectors receive information from different sources when evaluating the two.

Selection Tools

When considering external executives, selection committees rely more heavily on interviews, résumés, and references (although these three tools are used to collect information on both internal and external candidates). Committees are more likely to involve search firms to get information about external candidates. When considering internal candidates, selectors are more likely to rely on performance appraisals, succession plans, and subordinate reviews. (See Table 8.2.)

External candidates can control the information they provide in résumés and interviews, and to some extent, even in that obtained through search firms and references. Thus, the information gathered on external candidates is not only less extensive but also biased toward the positive. Information gathered on internal candidates (through performance appraisals, succession plans, and reviews, as well as by interacting with and watching candidates in their current positions, making presentations, and during meetings) is more balanced in terms of strengths and development needs. But this type of information is not usually available for external candidates. The result is a strong tendency to compare information obtained on external candidates with that obtained on internal candidates.

Table 8.2 Tools Used to Collect Information: Internal Versus External Hires.

Tools Used	Internal Executive Hired (Percentage)	External Executive Hired (Percentage)
Interview	74	97
Résumé	51	90
References	50	84
Search firm	12	56
Performance appraisal	68	12
Succession plan	33	7
Subordinate reviews	33	18

Note: N = 317; internal = 135; external = 182
Source: Sessa, Kaiser, Taylor, & Campbell, 1998.

In consequence, selectors often conclude that the external candidates "look" more positive, and they may be biased toward the external candidates. Executives told us such things as, "Companies are too hard on their internal candidates." One individual said, "I am aware that people tend to rate external candidates less candidly than internal ones. With internal candidates, you can talk with people who have worked with the candidate and you will receive an honest evaluation." One senior human resource executive who is aware of this tendency told us that he takes an active role during discussions to support insiders in order to make the evaluations more balanced.

Selection Information

Because different tools are used to gather information, different information is obtained on the candidates. For example, one selector we interviewed told us this about an unsuccessful hire, "The internal candidate was excluded on the basis of weak leadership skills. But externals were not assessed on leadership skills."

The reason why the executive is ultimately chosen from the pool of candidates differs between internal and external candidates in terms of hard-side characteristics, soft-side characteristics, and fit issues.

Hard-Side Information. As noted, external executives are brought in when they can offer skills that the organization specifically needs. They are more often chosen because of their business expertise, other knowledge, and technical expertise. Internal executives are more often chosen because of their demonstrated track record of success in the organization and for their own further development.

Soft-Side Information. External executives are chosen for their interpersonal skills—which, as we noted in Chapter Two, is problematic because selectors are really looking for relationship skills. These candidates are also often chosen because other candidates in the pool demonstrate a lack of skills (for example, a lack of communication skills). Internal executives are selected because they are known entities and have shown enough merit to qualify them for further development.

Fit. External executives are more often selected from the candidate pool because of their fit with the organization's culture or because other candidates in the pool do not fit. Internal executives are chosen because they are already known to the selectors.

In sum, because of the selection tools used, selectors seek and use different information on internal and external candidates. They gain less information on external candidates and that information may be biased toward the positive. They gain more (and more balanced) information on internal candidates. Because of the difference in the amount and type of information, selectors find external candidates more attractive. Despite these differences, it appears that selectors do try to assess external candidates on their hard-side and soft-side characteristics as well as their fit with the organization.

Treatment and Evaluation Once in the Position

According to our interviewees, there are no differences in the way new hires from outside the organization are managed once in the position compared with those who are hired internally. As we explained in Chapter Six, in general executives are not supported in any special way once they are in the new position. To their detriment, external hires are not any more likely to receive any sort of introduction to the organization—even though they are often brought in to aid the organization as part of a change effort. They do not receive any more support from their superior. And they are no more likely to be given intentional on- or off-the-job development. Interestingly, internals, who are often brought in for their own development, are similarly unlikely to receive any sort of support once they are in the position.

However, unlike the situation with treatment, there are differences in the ways in which external hires and internal hires are judged. During the first five months in the position external hires are less likely than internal hires to be judged on organizational results and their relationships. However, despite the lack of support given them, external hires are more likely to be judged more harshly when it comes to their actual performance. And the judgment is often made almost immediately after they accept the position.

The strengths and weaknesses of internal and external hires are also evaluated differently when it comes to hard side, soft side, and fit. Executives hired from the outside are more likely to be seen as having the technical expertise needed to accomplish the position requirements than internal hires are. This makes sense because external hires are specifically hired to bring in needed skills whereas internal hires are expected to develop these skills. However, although their interpersonal skills are gauged during their selection, external hires are seen as having problems with their peers. These findings suggest that external hires are expected to enter the organization as experts who do not need any introduction into the organization. They are expected to perform well on the job (that is, make the changes they were hired to make) and quickly, yet fit in with their peers—who perhaps themselves were seen as not having the expertise necessary to accomplish the job. In other words, although external hires are brought in as experts and expected to perform as experts, when they do so it may actually harm their relationships.

Executives hired from inside the company are more likely to be seen as having the specific knowledge the position needs than are those hired from the outside. They are also seen as generally getting along with others. Thus, despite being hired for developmental reasons, internal hires fare better and are more likely to be seen as having the hard skills, the soft skills, and the fit needed for the position.

In sum, external hires are hired to be perfect and punished for not being so. Internal hires are believed to be flawed and in need of development, so their performance is not expected to be perfect.

Different Paradigms

We have suggested that selectors use two different paradigms when selecting internal candidates and external candidates. Internal candidates are selected when the organization perceives that it is in a steady state. The candidates are seen through a developmental paradigm as an asset to be nurtured and developed. Selectors have a balanced view of their strengths and weaknesses. They are not expected to be perfect when on the job. Internal candidates do not "look" as positive as external candidates, who are brought in to be experts.

In contrast, external candidates are seen as assets that are acquired fully developed, with few weaknesses and with very little need for development. They are hired when the organization is in a state of change or believes it is missing something. They are expected to arrive on the job fully equipped to solve the organization's problems. They receive little support, yet are expected to perform well. They are hired for their expertise but are judged on their relationships. When they don't perform, they are often fired.

We believe this difference in view generally accounts for the greater success of internal hires. We also believe that we need to get beyond this dichotomy in the interest of greater success—regardless of the type of hire.

What does this discussion mean for internal and external selections? As we have seen, the process for bringing executives in from the outside is very different from the process of hiring an internal executive. That difference is a liability, but there are several things an organization can do to resolve the situation.

Combine the Development and Selection Paradigms

Assess both what the candidate can do for the organization and what the organization must do to support and develop the candidate. Do both whether the new hire has come from the outside or from inside the organization.

Do Not Overestimate the Capabilities of External Executives

In addition, do not underestimate the capabilities of executives inside the organization. Keep in mind that you may be seeing only the "beauty marks" of the external candidates and the "warts" of the internal candidates. In reality, external candidates may not be better than the others. Know that you have more information available to assess internal candidates. Realize that external executives have developmental needs too.

Try to Use the Same Information Sources for All Candidates

As much as possible, rely on the same sources of information for all candidates. For example, if you use a search firm to find external candidates, use them to assess potential internal candidates as well.

This does not mean that you should ignore performance appraisals, succession plans, and subordinate reviews when considering an internal candidate. But realize that this information provides you with a different picture of your internal candidates. Performance appraisals, succession plans, and subordinate reviews provide a more "balanced" view of the individual, giving you both strengths and weaknesses.

At Maytag, top-level executives treat internal and external candidates the same. They carefully put both internal and external candidates through the same external assessment process and even wait to interview internal candidates until the external candidates arrive for their interviews.

Clarify Fit

Although it is admirable that selectors are aware that fit issues are of high importance for external hires, they are not doing a stellar job of assessing them. Until a better understanding of fit is developed, organizations must be as precise as possible when they say an executive "fits" or doesn't fit.

Give All New Executives a Socialization Period

New executives need time to "learn" the new job, become acquainted with their new roles, meet their new associates, and generally get comfortable. This is especially true when an executive is brought in to make a change and must also learn a new culture and develop relationships with new people. Earle Malden, president of Bell-South Enterprises, when asked about the discrepant success rate of external and internal hires, told us,

> Internal hires have a great success rate in our company. From my own experience, I see that the company organism has in it a certain way of doing things. It doesn't take kindly to change. Those outsiders who are able to be successful need two things. First, they need

the political skills to adequately conform their own style to the need of the bureaucracy. There is a certain diplomacy associated with that. It takes a lot of talent to integrate yourself into the new business. Second, it takes a CEO and senior-level team to steadfastly support the outsider. I cannot emphasize enough the tone and the flavor of that support. One of the biggest tensions that you see with outsiders around our senior tables is that they are more impatient than our insiders. They have a sense of urgency against the old way of doing things.

Do Not Develop a Hiring Strategy That Favors One Candidate Type

Unless there is a strategic reason for doing so, do not develop a hiring strategy that favors either internal or external candidates. Hiring exclusively from the inside may limit the fresh ideas and perspectives an organization needs to survive and adapt. Hiring exclusively from the outside reduces opportunities for internal candidates and weakens their commitment to the organization. Ulrich and Lake (1990) have shown that organizations tend to have optimum innovation, performance, and flexibility with an 80–20 ratio: 80 percent hired from within and 20 percent from outside the immediate business unit. Your company needs to develop its own ratio of internal and external hires depending on its specific needs.

Summary

In this chapter we discussed a paradox: organizations are increasingly turning to the outside to hire top-level executives, yet those hired from the outside do not fare as well as insiders once on the job. We suggest that there are three reasons for this situation.

First, many organizations today are in a state of change. When in a state of change, top-level executive selectors are more likely to look to the outside for someone with the experiences, skills, knowledge, or other needed credentials that the selectors perceive are missing from their organization. In contrast, when organizations are *not* perceived to be in a state of change, selectors believe they need "more of the same" and they often view the open position as developmental.

Second, during the decision-making process, selectors find that external executives look better than internal executives because they do not have access to the same information on both. Overall, there is less information about external executives and the information available tends to be positive. More information, both formal and informal, is available about internal candidates, and that information is typically balanced in terms of strengths and weaknesses.

Finally, there are different expectations for external and internal hires. External hires are seen through a selection paradigm. They are selected because the organization is in a state of change and needs something new—and the external executive is perceived as able to fill that specific need. In contrast, internal executives are seen through a developmental paradigm. There is an understanding that they bring needed strengths to the position but also that they have areas that need development. We suggest combining selection and development into one paradigm in the selection process. Executives should not be selected unless they bring needed strengths to the position. Yet all executives, whether internal or external, need to be developed in some areas in order to be successful in the position.

Chapter Nine

A Summary of the System

The plan we have developed dovetails with the selection systems many companies already have in place. It is not meant to usurp them but rather to improve them, because it targets the decision makers. The following questions and recommendations summarize the steps in our system and help put them in perspective. This chapter is not exactly a checklist, but it can serve as a quick overview of the steps that were proceeded through in more detail in the previous chapters. We recommend referring to this chapter during selection meetings and to gain a quick understanding of the system. Refer to the chapters noted for details.

Choose the Selection Committee (Chapter Three)

Be deliberate about forming the selection committee. The individuals chosen to make the choice are almost as important as the individual chosen to fill the position. Provide guidance. Spell out the committee's responsibilities and how the final decision is to be made. Follow these steps to help select the people who will assist in the decision-making process:

- Use a team to make the decision.
- Use the same people throughout the decision process.
- Design the selection committee for best results. Include on the team a variety of people who will work with the candidates. Include subordinates and customers.

- Take into account team dynamics, especially in terms of hierarchy and politics. Intentionally choose team members who have demonstrated an ability to put aside their own agendas for the good of the organization and who will listen to diverse viewpoints.

- Carefully spell out the committee's responsibilities: ensuring that the search mechanisms or processes develop a sufficient number of candidates; ensuring that the candidates identified possess the required characteristics and experience; ensuring that the committee looks deep enough inside the organization; making a decision about whether to promote from within or hire from outside; keeping an open mind and getting advice from others outside the immediate committee; and holding a minority opinion, even if others on the committee agree on a candidate.

Map the Challenge (Chapter Four)

Take a holistic look at the organization, the job, and the measures of success before you begin the search. Doing this ensures that all important information will be considered, different perspectives will be heard, all constituents will understand what the new hire is expected to do, and everyone involved will be in agreement. Create a picture of the ideal candidate that will serve different functions throughout the selection process: to help recruit candidates, to provide the "ideal" to which each candidate will be compared, and to communicate with the chosen executive what he or she is supposed to do and how he or she will be evaluated once on the job.

This step can be broken down into three ministeps: *assess the organization, outline job requirements,* and *outline candidate requirements.* Here are the questions for each ministep:

Assess the Organization

- What do our vision, our strategy, our goals, and our structure say we need?

- How does our organization do things; how do we want to do things in the future? What does this suggest we need in hiring a new executive?
- What do we value?
- How are we unique?
- Where are our biggest issues going to be in the next few years? (You may need to pay attention to globalization; increased competition; economic, political, and social upheaval; temporary or ad hoc relationships through alliances, joint ventures, and partnerships; a flatter organization; management of processes rather than units or people; a learning organization; temporary employees.)
- Where are we weak? Do we want to improve in these areas?
- Where are we strong? Do we want to be even stronger in these areas?
- What are our climate, culture, and leadership styles?
- What kind of person do we want to work with?
- What kind of person would enjoy working here, would do well in this sort of environment?
- What does it mean to be successful in this organization?

Outline Job Requirements

- What are the goals of this position?
- What are the major tasks and activities—both "work" and "people management" tasks and activities?
- How does this position relate to other positions? Is there anything in particular we should keep in mind about the person who is currently in the position (for example, working style)?
- What are the strengths of this team or department? Does this position require the executive to have these strengths as well?

- What are the weaknesses of this team or department? What skills does the new hire need in order to help rectify these weaknesses?

- What will it mean to be successful in this position?

Outline Candidate Requirements

- Based on our organizational needs and job requirements, what are the experience and background requirements for the candidates?

- What knowledge, skills, abilities, or characteristics are needed to do the work? To survive in our organization?

- What are the educational requirements? Are certain degrees or licenses needed?

- Do we need these candidate characteristics: vision, wisdom, courage, trustworthiness, ability to mentor, ability to take risks, decisiveness, charisma, relationship with the outside world, ability to take a broad view?

- What qualities do executives need to have in order to be successful in this organization?

Recruit the Right Candidates (Chapter Five)

Gather a qualified pool of candidates. If you do not take this step, then your task will be incredibly difficult, even impossible. Consider both the organization's point of view and the candidates' point of view when doing so.

To recruit effectively from the organization's point of view, ask yourself the following questions:

- Have we included both good information about ourselves and realistic expectations in our materials so that we can give candidates a realistic job preview? Did we use the information that we gathered on organizational needs, position, and candidate requirements?

- Are we being realistic about our candidate requirements so that there is a viable pool of candidates?

- What is our bench strength? And who is next in the succession plan? Is that person ready?

- Do we already have executives who have the needed expertise for our organizational needs and position requirements?

- Do we want or need to look at outside candidates? Is there a particular candidate we would like to recruit?

- Have we asked knowledgeable insiders and outsiders for recommendations for candidates? Have we put advertisements in useful locations? Have we done our own research or hired a search firm to find candidates for us?

- Should we consider other candidates we have been impressed with?

- Are there any consultants we have worked with and know well who might be a fit for this job?

- Have we considered all sources? Have we properly tapped into a variety of different populations?

- Do we have enough candidates to make a good selection? Have we cast our net wide enough to get the top-quality candidates yet narrow enough so that we aren't getting those who would not fit?

- Why would a smart, energetic, ambitious executive want to work for us rather than going somewhere else?

Be aware that candidates will have their own questions, such as these:

- Do I want this job?
- Is this a prestigious or attractive organization? Does it have good financials? And is it unlikely to be taken over in the foreseeable future?

- Is this a stable job or one I will use as a stepping-stone into another position?
- Will this mean moving? Do I or my family want to move? Will the organization be supportive in helping us move?
- What are the pay, the benefits, the fringe benefits?
- Is this team made up of top-quality individuals with whom I would like to work?
- Is it worth the bother to jump into the pool?
- Am I getting a real picture of the organization and the position? Or am I going to be shocked when I understand the real expectations once on the job?
- What's in it for me?
- Do my values fit with this organization?
- Does my style of working fit with the culture?
- Will I be working in a climate that is supportive and with people I will enjoy working with?
- Who will help me learn to fit into this new culture?
- Will there be ongoing support from the organization to help me succeed? Are the criteria for success clear?
- Will I be able to make a positive contribution?
- Are there any hidden agendas I need to be careful about?
- What is my sense of how the other executives are treated and how they feel about the company?

Make the Selection Decision (Chapter Six)

Only after accomplishing the first three steps should you enter the heart of the selection process: that is, make the match. If you have done a good job creating an outline for the "ideal" candidate, selecting a top-notch selection committee, and recruiting high-quality candidates, this process should go smoothly.

Take a Disciplined Approach

Make sure you are gathering the information that matches the organizational assessment and the job and candidate requirements.

Fit the Selection Tools to the Information You Need

To assess factual and measurable attributes—hard-side skills—get information from interviews, references, résumés, and 360-degree assessments. Tailor your questions specifically to the skills you are trying to assess. (For example, if one of your candidate requirements is for someone who can turn around a failing division, ask candidates and their references to describe specific situations, actions, and results relating to their experience with turnarounds.) For soft-side skills, use psychological assessments, subordinate and customer feedback, and 360-degree feedback that is geared toward the specific soft skills you are interested in assessing. (For example, if inspiring trust is a quality you are looking for, talk to subordinates and customers about how they feel about the candidate.)

Treat All Candidates Similarly

Be sure not to treat internal and external candidates differently, and make sure you get similar information on both. It is difficult enough to compare candidates to the ideal candidate and to one another when you have the same information on each. If you have a different set of information on each candidate, making a fair comparison is nearly impossible. If you are satisfied that you have done a good job spelling out the necessary organizational needs and job and candidate requirements and have actually gained that information from each of the potential candidates, *and if your intuition has been useful in the past,* then by all means use your intuition to help you make the final decision. You are an expert in decision making. To the extent that your expertise is based on logical and well-founded experience, then so is your intuition. But if you are choosing an executives you feel comfortable with because of emotional reasons or because he or she is "like" you demographically, or if you personally are stressed, are being dishonest with yourself, or have personal gain in the decision, then don't rely on your intuition.

Use Your Intuition Cautiously

When you do find yourself relying on gut feelings, ask yourself the following questions to make sure that you have consulted all possible sources of information first:

- Have we asked other people for information or what their impressions are? Are we including this information or discounting it?
- Has our initial impression of this person changed as we have gotten to know him?
- What have we learned new about the person that confirms or disconfirms our intuition?
- What kinds of judgments are we making that are actually inferences that we have not backed up with hard data or asked about directly?
- Does this person make any of us uncomfortable? Why?
- How different is this person from the rest of the team? Are those differences that we are looking for?
- Is there information out there that challenges our intuition (not just information that reinforces it)?

After the Selection Is Made (Chapter Seven)

Selection is not over the moment the selected candidate accepts the position. Develop and support the candidate to ensure success. Prepare the individual for the organization and the position. And prepare the organization for the new executive. Consider the following guidelines:

- Provide the new hire with assimilation and integration during the first six months, helping him or her learn the ropes, transmitting the culture, and explaining the politics and power dynamics.
- Prepare the organization to accept the new hire—especially if he or she is expected to be a change agent.
- Provide all executives with continued development. Remember, organizations change, jobs change, coworkers change, and the new hire changes over time. What works well in one situation may be a weakness in the next.

Consider the Differences Between Internal and External Selection Processes (Chapter Eight)

Internal selection processes differ from external selection processes. Plan for this. Here are some suggestions for handling a search that includes both internal and external candidates.

- Combine the development and selection paradigms for both internal and external candidates. Assess both what the candidate can do for the organization and what the organization must do to support and develop the candidate.
- Do not assume that external candidates are better than internal ones. Understand that you have more information on internal candidates. Realize that external executives have developmental areas, too.
- In general, use the same people and the same information sources for information on all candidates and to make decisions about them. If you use a search firm for external candidates, use it also to assess potential internal candidates. Use performance appraisals, succession plans, and subordinate

reviews when considering an internal candidate but realize that this information provides you with a different picture of your internal candidates—a more "balanced" view, including both strengths and weaknesses.

- Be as precise as possible when you say an executive fits or doesn't fit your organization.

- Once the new hire is in the position, allow her a socialization period and time to "learn" the new job, meet new associates, and generally get comfortable. Do this especially if she must also learn a new culture and develop relationships with new people.

- Do not develop a hiring strategy that excludes either internal or external candidates. Hiring exclusively from the inside may limit fresh ideas and perspectives that your organization needs to survive and adapt. Hiring exclusively from the outside reduces opportunities for the internal candidates and weakens their commitment to the organization.

Summary

This chapter concludes the review of our findings from our research to date. In the next and final chapter, we discuss a compelling idea that has developed from our research: executive selection is not a stand-alone process; it must fit into other organizational systems and into the organization's assumptions about leadership in general.

Chapter Ten

Selection and Your Organization

Two Final Thoughts

The message of this book is that the people you choose to lead your company make up its basic building blocks for success. The best strategies in the world are useless if you don't have people who can execute them. Think about high-performing sports teams. Coaches are very strategic and intentional about the talent they recruit, and they recruit different kinds of talent for different positions. Together, all the players combine to create a high-performing team. What spectators see are a team's wins and losses—and an organization's wins and losses. Yet coaches—and astute top executives—spend a great deal of time in behind-the-scenes activities such as recruiting high-quality talent. Coaches know they will never be able to create a championship team without the right people. Organizations are the same. They will not be able to succeed in this competitive, changing world unless they have the right talent.

In this volume, we have built a case for how a complex set of environmental factors is making selection more difficult and more important in organizations today. Organizations have to shift strategy rapidly. Global competition has become more intense, increasing the need for adaptability and responsiveness. Shortened product cycles and more demanding customers have necessitated more urgency and speed. Downsizing has caused the talent pool to shrink. Our research has shown that using a team-based and systematic selection process at the top of organizations will improve the success of their top executives.

But selection is not a stand-alone process; it does not occur in a vacuum. Rather, it occurs within a complex organism. Selectors need to have a realistic view of the whole organization, how its systems function, and how they affect executive selection. In addition, selectors need to understand the organization's prevailing view of leadership and how it may affect and be affected by the selection of top-level executives. The information in this chapter represents the Center for Creative Leadership's next steps in systemic leadership development, of which executive selection is one part. The focus of systemic leadership development is on building sustainable leadership capacity as well as creative and capable leaders.

Organizational Systems

Selection occurs in the context of four interlocking organizational systems that are part of all organizations and that we will describe in the following paragraphs: *production*, *control*, *learning*, and *rewards*. Top-level executives work continually to integrate and align these systems but at the same time change and develop them to respond to changing environmental forces.

The four systems themselves each contain formal and informal aspects. Formal aspects include recorded rules, policies, procedures, strategies, and plans. Informal aspects include employees' interpretations of the formal aspects and knowledge of "how things really get done around here."

Production

The production system is responsible for what the organization does—whether it is to produce actual goods, intangible goods (knowledge work), or services. This system deals with the structure of the work, the resources available to accomplish the work, and the allocation of those resources. But production alone does not make the organization. As John Smale, chairman of the board of General Motors, said in a speech to the leaders of GM worldwide: "A great company truly is a living thing. It grows or it stagnates or it dies—from generation to generation to generation. There is the never-ending challenge of constantly reinventing what you do." Companies die because managers focus exclusively on producing goods and services and forget that their organization is a community of human beings.

Control

The control system deals with directing, regulating, and coordinating organizational activities. This system determines how decisions get made in organizations and who makes decisions. Effective decision making is critical for the organization to take any action and to execute its strategies. The task of executive selection—and all staffing activities—falls to this system. Executive selection is, at its most basic, a result of a company's decision-making processes. The information presented in this book derives from the informal side of the control system—executives talked to us about how selection is really accomplished in their organizations, not about the formal succession plans, policies, and procedures.

Learning

The learning system deals with both information and education—that is, how knowledge and skills are acquired, disseminated, and used. This system determines how information flows from those who have it to those who need it to do their work. The learning system encompasses all training and education systems and all information systems, such as management systems and information systems. It also encompasses executive development, which we at CCL link closely with executive selection.

Rewards

The fourth system is the reward system. Rewards include the tangible (for example, salary) and intangible (for example, perks). The reward system determines who and what gets rewarded. It is through the reward system that we can get the clearest idea of organizational values, beliefs, and opinions about what is important and what is not important.

Depending on the organization, these four systems interact to varying degrees. For example, in poorly integrated organizations, top-level executives may affirm that they want to drive decision making down to the lowest possible level of the organization (using such terms as "empowerment") yet have no learning system in place (that is, no system for those who are lower in the organization to attain or develop the skills and knowledge they need to make decisions), no rewards for either making decisions or allowing decision making to take place at low levels, and no allowances in the production systems for the decisions to have an effect.

Although the actual executive selection process is housed in the control system, the executive chosen affects all four systems. Therefore, the more aware the selection committee is of both the formal and informal aspects of the four systems and how they interact in the organization, the more conscious the committee can be in selecting an executive who fits with, can enhance, or can change the systems as needed.

Changing Views of Leadership

In addition to these four systems, organizations also have prevailing or implicit views of leadership. The better these prevailing views are understood, the more likely the executive chosen can enhance or change the leadership style.

Leadership involves four main tasks: setting direction, facing challenges, creating alignment, and maintaining commitment. But how leadership is actually enacted varies depending on the organization and changes over time within the same organization.

For example, in the past few years, the organizational literature has become rife with new leadership terminology, words such as *distributed leadership*, *leadership teams*, *top management teams*, *cross-functional teams*, *adhocracies*, and *flatter organizational structures*. To carry out the promise of these concepts, organizations are coming to a new understanding of what it means to lead. Leadership can be seen as evolving from a *personal dominance principle* to an *interpersonal influence principle* to a *relational sensemaking principle*. Each of these principles encompasses and builds on the previous one.

Personal Dominance Principle

According to the personal dominance principle, leadership is housed within a leader. The leader goes first and is strong and smart. He or she provides protection and guidance, defines values, and explains what is important. The leader controls and limits conflict. Leadership (that is, setting direction, facing challenges, creating alignment, and maintaining commitment) is what the leader does.

Interpersonal Influence Principle

According to the interpersonal influence principle, influencing others is more effective than personal dominance. The leader influences followers through reason, knowledge, and shared information. To do this, the leader must understand the followers and what is important to them. This allows for the beginning of a two-way interaction between the leader and the follower. Leadership is seen as social negotiation between leader and follower, with the leader influencing the followers more than the followers influence the leader.

Relational Sense-Making Principle

According to the relational sense-making principle, leadership evolves so that it is no longer inherent in a single person. In addition, leadership is no longer synonymous with authority. Terms such as *leader* and *follower* represent only one way of participating in leadership but no longer define it completely. Instead, acts of leadership (again, setting direction, facing challenges, creating alignment, and maintaining commitment) are constructed within and between people as they interact. People participate in leadership together at every organizational level, and leadership can take many recognizable forms. This way of defining leadership allows anyone in the organization to practice leadership, although accountability is still housed within a specified set of individuals. Relational sense-making leadership empowers people in organizations to move quickly in response to changing environments. This style of leadership seems to fit well in today's information society.

In any given organization, these principles of leadership are married to the four organizational systems. For example, a reward system that follows the personal dominance principle awards those who climb the executive ladder, and the reward scheme clearly differentiates leaders from followers (offering such perks as the special parking space, the corner office, and so on). A reward system that follows the interpersonal influence principle still rewards leaders differently than nonleaders, but there is some recognition and reward for those who work best with followers and for followers who are most helpful to leaders. Under the relational sense-making principle, an organization can explicitly construct different rewards for those who are willing to climb the executive hierarchy (and thus assume more accountability), those who wish to remain individual contributors, those who cross functional lines, and those who work in support roles—recognizing that leadership occurs in many different arenas and in many different forms.

The better selectors understand their own views of leadership and those espoused through the different organizational systems (which may vary in degree of alignment with each other), the more explicit the selection process can be made. The chosen executive will have an impact on the way leadership is viewed in the organization. In an extreme case, if an executive who espouses the personal dominance perspective is chosen, that may hinder an organization in its attempts to put in place team-based organizational structures. And if an executive who sees leadership from a relational sense-making point of view is chosen, he or she may become frustrated in an organization that is structured to reward the personal dominance style of leadership.

Summary

As this chapter explains, our ongoing research is beginning to focus on helping executives gain a better understanding of how their organizational systems and prevailing beliefs about leadership all work together to enhance or inhibit leadership selection and development in their organizations. Selection occurs in a complex organizational environment. Like a living, breathing organism, each part interacts with all the other parts to make it the unique place that it is. The better top-level executives understand the complexities of their organizational environment and the broad impact of the decisions they make, the better the decisions—including the selection of other top-level executives—will be.

Appendix A:
Interview Questionnaire and Protocol

The interview study took place from 1993 to 1995. The 498 executives interviewed were all CEOs and two levels down participating in CCL's Leadership at the Peak training program. The study had two parts. On the first day, executives received a questionnaire and an explanation of the interview that they would be participating in. On the second day, trained researchers conducted in-depth interviews with the executives, each usually lasting an hour. For a full description of the study, see Sessa, Kaiser, Taylor, and Campbell (1998), *Executive Selection: A Research Report on What Works and What Doesn't*.

Questionnaire

Please pick a successful (unsuccessful) executive selection decision that occurred at your current company for discussion in the interview. It should be a specific selection decision in which you were involved, where the target position was the CEO or two levels below. Please provide the following information for this incident:

a. What was the position to be filled?

b. What level was the position?
_____ CEO
_____ One level below
_____ Two levels below
_____ Other _____

c. What happened to the previous incumbent in the position?
 _____ New position
 _____ Incumbent left organization voluntarily
 _____ Incumbent left organization involuntarily
 _____ Incumbent promoted
 _____ Incumbent moved laterally
 _____ Other _____

d. What was your role in the selection decision?

e. What was your relationship to the position to be filled? (check all that apply)
 _____ My subordinate
 _____ A peer
 _____ My boss
 _____ A member of my team
 _____ Other _____

f. How many people were directly involved in making the decision? _____

g. How many women were directly involved in the decision-making process? _____

h. How many minorities were directly involved in the decision-making process? _____

i. Who was involved?

	In the decision making	In providing information
Chair of the board	_____	_____
Board of directors	_____	_____
CEO/president/ business owner	_____	_____
Superior of the position	_____	_____
Superior—two up	_____	_____

Peers of superior   ____   ____
Former incumbent   ____   ____
Future subordinates
  of position   ____   ____
Peers of the position   ____   ____
HR department   ____   ____
Potential "customers"   ____   ____
  of the position
Other _____   ____   ____

j. Number of months since selection decision: ____

k. Were you in your current job at the time of the selection decision? ____ Yes ____ No
If *no*, please provide the following information about you as of the time of the selection decision:
Organization _____
Your position or functional area _____
How long had you been in that position? _____
Your level in the organization_____
How long had you been at that level? _____
How long had you been at that organization? _____

l. What was the purpose of the selection? (Check all that apply.)
____ Sustaining and continuing the organization
____ A developmental placement
____ A start-up
____ A turnaround
____ Other _____

m. Tell us about the person who was selected:
Race _____ Age ____ Sex ____
____ Internal candidate
____ External candidate
____ Succession plan participant
Functional background _____

n. Tell us about the other candidates:
    Number of candidates seriously considered for the job: _____

Sex (M/F)	Age	External Candidate (yes/no)	Functional Background	Minority Candidate (yes/no)
1._____	_____	_____	_____	_____
2._____	_____	_____	_____	_____
3._____	_____	_____	_____	_____
4._____	_____	_____	_____	_____
5._____	_____	_____	_____	_____

o. What methods did you use to obtain information about the
    various candidates? (Check all that apply in the first column,
    then rank those you checked, in order of importance with 1
    being the most important, in the second column.)

Method	Used	Importance
Resumes	_____	_____
Interviews	_____	_____
References	_____	_____
Peer reviews	_____	_____
Reviews from current subordinates	_____	_____
Performance appraisals	_____	_____
Assessment center results	_____	_____
Executive search firms	_____	_____
Succession plans	_____	_____
Tests:		
Personality	_____	_____
Ability	_____	_____
Other (Please list below.)		
_____	_____	_____
_____	_____	_____
_____	_____	_____

p. Where is the person now?
    _____ Left company—involuntary
    _____ Left company—voluntary

____ Demoted
____ Still in job
____ Different job, same level
____ Promoted

For the top positions in your organization (CEO and two levels below):

q. How successful is the selection process? (on a scale of 1 to 5, 1 being very unsuccessful and 5 being very successful) ____

r. What is the hit rate (percent of selections that prove to be successful)?
External percent   ____
Internal percent   ____
Overall percent   ____

s. What proportion of the top positions have been filled from external sources over the last four years? ____

t. How has the proportion of external selections in top positions changed over the last four years ?
____ Large increase
____ Moderate increase
____ No change
____ Moderate decrease
____ Substantial decrease

u. How many top-level selections have you participated in over the past four years? ____

Areas to Be Covered in the Interview

The interview will focus on the selection decision you described above. We will seek more in-depth information in the following areas. Any thought you can give to these questions prior to the interview will make it more productive and interesting for you.

1. How did you know that the selection decision was successful (unsuccessful)? Specifically, what was it about the person's performance, accomplishments, relationships, etc., that caused the person to be considered successful (unsuccessful) in this position?

2. What factors contributed to this person's success (lack of success)?

3. Who was involved in the selection process?

4. Was this an open search? Did you specifically target internal/external candidates? Why did you choose this strategy?

5. What kind of information did the people involved want about the candidate?

6. Was information desired that couldn't be obtained?

7. Who made the decision?

8. Why was this person selected? How did he/she compare with the other contenders for the job? In hindsight, were there better people for the job? If so, why weren't they selected?

9. What was different about this selection decision, compared with more "typical" cases, that made this one particularly successful (unsuccessful)?

The Interview Protocols: The Successful Selection Decision

Thank you for recalling a specific successful selection decision and filling out the questionnaire. It will help move our interview along.

I hope you will agree to permit CCL to use the information you provide in its research on executive selection. This is a voluntary decision on your part, of course. This statement gives the terms of the agreement (to allow use of the data for research purposes). It stipulates that all information about individuals is confidential, and that we list the participating organizations in our reports only if they wish to be included as supporters of our research.

Interviewer: Answer any questions the participant may have. Encourage research participation, but do not pressure reluctant participants. If they reject use of the data for research, simply thank them for considering our request. Should the interviewee agree, have her/him sign the form. Should they later wish to keep something out of the report, or change their minds about allowing use of the data, honor their wishes.

Interviewer: What follows is a suggested structure for the interview and some probes; but we expect you to go with the flow. At the outset, be sure that the interviewee has selected a specific selection decision.

Performance of Target

Think of the successful selection decision that was made in your organization that you discussed in your presession packet. Discuss why this selection was successful.

Why considered successful? Want specifics (e.g., results, performance, relationships, etc.).

- Specifically, what was it about the person's performance, results, or relationships that caused the person to be labeled a success in this position?

What were the important contextual factors (e.g., difficulty of the job, environmental stability, boss, etc.)?

- What were the important contextual factors about the job that contributed to the success of the person?
- What was done to prepare the person and the organization for the transplant?

What were the person's critical strengths and weaknesses?

- What were the person's critical strengths that made her/him successful in this job?
- What were the person's main weaknesses and how did he/she cope with them in this situation?
- In hindsight, was there a better person for the job? Why wasn't he/she selected?

Organizational Assessment

What were the organization's needs and strategy?/Purpose of the selection? (*Interviewers, we are trying to see if there was any attempt to link the position requirements to the strategy of the organization, without leading the interviewee.*)

- What were the organization's needs and business strategy at the time the selection was taking place?
- What was going on in the organization at the time that might have influenced the selection?
- What was the purpose of the selection? (organizational goals, development of the person, etc.)

Specs or requirements of the job: What had to be achieved?

- What were the requirements of the position? (*What was the person expected to accomplish on the job? This is different from a person's characteristics. Examples might be start a new department, improve competitive position, introduce a new technology. Get a job description.*)
- Who defined what the position was to be?
- How much time was spent assessing the organization's needs and defining the position?

How explicit were these assessments?

- On a scale of 1 being very vague and 5 being very explicit, how explicit were the needs, definitions, and requirements of this position?

Candidate Requirements

Individual requirements. (*Interviewer, we want specifics; e.g., if the participant says track record, what were they looking for in the track record?*)

- What did the candidate need to be capable of doing?
- What skills, dispositions, values, competencies were desired? (*These two probes are aimed at identifying the characteristics and demographics of the person sought. They might include educational, professional, or functional background; track record; certain skills [e.g., communication, intelligence, decision making, etc.]; personality characteristics [e.g., aggressiveness, emotional stability, ethics, etc.]; to name a few possibilities.*)

How explicit were these requirements?

- On a scale of 1 being very vague and 5 being very explicit, how explicit were the skills, dispositions, values, and competencies that you required?

Breadth of Search

What was the selection strategy? (External = outside the organization, internal = inside the organization. If you are uncertain, describe the situation in detail and why you are unsure.)

- Was this an open search? Did you specifically target internals or externals? Why was this selection strategy used? If an *internal* candidate: Does the organization have a succession planning system? Was this candidate a product of the succession plan? If an *external* candidate: Why was there a decision to go outside? Was a search firm used?

What types of information were considered most important?

- What kind of information did the people involved in the selection want about the candidates? (*Interviewer, you might review techniques used as indicated in the questionnaire. What kinds of information were they trying to get from these techniques?*)
- Which techniques (interview, tests, etc.) were most helpful? Least helpful? Why?
- Was there any information the group wanted but couldn't get?
- What were the deciding factors in selecting this particular candidate?

Information about the other candidates

- Who were the other contenders for the job? (*Interviewer, part of this information should be on the questionnaire form.*)
- What were the deciding factors in rejecting these candidates?

Group Decision-Making Process

What was the interviewee's role?

- What was your role in the selection process? What was your role in the decision?

How was the final decision made?

- What was important in making the decision?
- How was the selection decision made? (consensus, chair decided, etc.)
- Was approval from above needed?

What were concerns/expectations about person selected?

- What were the concerns/expectations about the person when selected?

How long did the process take?

- How much organizational time would you estimate was spent on the selection decision?
- How long did the selection process take from the beginning to the end?

How structured was the decision-making process?

- Using a scale of 1 being very unstructured to 5 being very structured, how structured was the selection decision process?

In what ways was this selection process atypical for your organization?

- What were the two or three major differences between this case and other "typical" selection cases? (*Interviewer, continue to probe here regarding similarities to other external or internal selections.*)
- Why did this selection decision go so well?

General

Interviewee's view of:

- What are the critical issues in executive selection that you think top executives would find useful/like to know more about?
- What are the two things that would help you the most in making executive selection decisions?
- What could be done during LAP to help you do a better job in selection? Or as a candidate for a job?

Appendix B: Description of the Peak Selection Simulation

In early 1993, the Center for Creative Leadership began working on a research-training simulation to give senior-level executives a realistic experience in handling team selection decisions and to provide research data on decision making by executive teams. In November 1995 this simulation was installed as a major component of Leadership at the Peak, a development program for senior-level executives.

Our goal was to create a context-rich experience through which senior executives could grapple with selection issues very similar to those they face in their home organizations. In this process they would confront difficulties typical of decision making by any individual or team, regardless of task. We wanted to create a research-training simulation that would allow us tight control over variables that would satisfy multiple research perspectives on choice behavior while at the same time furnishing us with real examples of how executives and executive teams make selection decisions. The research would be designed around the issues of context, process, and people. Is organizational context considered in making selection decisions? What individual and team processes lead to the most effective decisions? What leadership characteristics influence those outcomes?

The training simulation would accommodate certain realities of senior-level teams: a differential distribution of information because no one individual knows everything needed to make the best decision; an external criterion that leaves no doubt as to desired outcome; and high stakes. The learning points for the executives would focus on both individual and team choice behavior, as well as principles of executive selection.

Development of the Simulation

When a phenomenon is not well understood (in this case, executive selection) the realism of the simulation needs to be high so that relevant and irrelevant variables can be distinguished. Our focus on developing this realism included the following:

Field Surveys

Field interviews with search firms and senior executives gave us numerous ideas about executive character and what is actually considered during executive selection. For the most part, our candidates are modeled on well-known senior executives, each with a distinct personality, personal background, and qualifications.

Organizational Environment

The company background was drawn from Looking Glass, a large-scale behavioral simulation already used at the Center for Creative Leadership. Created in the late 1970s and updated in 1991, Looking Glass is an exceptionally accurate and detailed simulated company that was based on a close look at products and technology, plant visits, an understanding of basic manufacturing processes, interviews with glass industry managers, a scouring of trade journals, and a "feel" for the industry's environmental problems.

Solution to the Simulation

To crystallize learning and provide criteria for measurement, we established a preferred ranking of candidates in descending order of fit. To assume all candidates are equal would invalidate the framework for selection; there would be no best decision to make. In the world of executive selection, all choices are not equally good. The world of executive selection is hit-or-miss; if you didn't get it right, you got it wrong.

The solution we designed into the simulation was based on an organizational and job assessment of both the company and the division, specification of candidate requirements, and assessment of the four candidates, matching the qualifications of the candidates to the organizational needs. All materials, including the candidate information, were developed and written based on this model. Candidates would display strengths, weaknesses, and derailment factors and would vary in fit to this particular organization and job.

Because they were all the "cream of the crop," each candidate was outstanding in one respect or another. One resembled the typical participant in the Leadership at the Peak program. Another fit the current "solution" reported so widely in the popular press: the outsider brought in to shake up the organization. A third candidate was the "quiet, nonadministrative sleeper." The fourth was a highly competent, creative renegade who had derailed during his time with Looking Glass.

We then called on experts to verify our solution. This small panel performed organizational and job assessments, outlined the candidate specifications, and assessed the candidates in terms of those specifications. Two caveats should be noted. First, unlike Leadership at the Peak participants who work against a deadline, these verifying experts spent as much time as needed in reading the materials. Second, the experts were not given the information through multimedia presentation; instead, they used written materials that they could read and reread as much and as often as they wanted. They did in fact verify the design solution as the "best" solution available, given the organizational requirements and the position to be filled.

Training Sequence

Prior to their arrival to begin the five-day program, participants are provided with extensive information about the company, Looking Glass, Inc. This preprogram work includes a brochure describing the company's products, history, and a proposed ten-year strategic plan. (Although participants are not involved with the problems of the original Looking Glass simulation used at CCL, they are never far from the world of a glass company: its finances, its color, its competitive challenges, its products, its revered history. Looking Glass faces an uncertain future. Competitors have taken important business. The draft ten-year plan proposes fundamental changes: greater global involvement, the sale of one division, and more. An investment banking firm in London and a New York management consultant believe Looking Glass will lose position if major changes are not made.) Participants are also provided a one-page resume for each of the four candidates. They are asked not to discuss this material.

After an introduction to the simulation on the first afternoon, the participants are greeted on video by the CEO of Looking Glass, who sets out their task: to choose a president for the Advanced Products Division. This division manufactures fiber optics, capacitors, and liquid crystal display glass. Because a major refocusing of Advanced Products is proposed in the ten-year plan, the position of president will, to a great extent, be a new job. Thus, the candidate selected must be capable of redefining the job.

Following a tutorial on the computer search program, each participant is given one hour to examine the four candidates through interactive multimedia presentation. Sitting before a monitor, the participants are presented a screen menu that provides all the candidate information. By operating a computer mouse, they can listen to and watch an interview of each candidate, with a variety of questions asked of all candidates, listen to audiotapes of opinions about the candidate (both solicited and unsolicited), look at the resumes, look at HR information, and look at information compiled about each candidate by a search firm. This CD-ROM multimedia presentation does not force a linear, sequential interaction. Event-driven programming coupled with TV-quality video adapts to each individual's learning style. The user, not the developer, determines the sequence of events. Through an "intelligent" database, the computer tracks how long the user has spent on each piece of information and the sequence in which he or she looked at the information. (For an in-depth description of the individual search portion of this research, see Deal, Sessa, & Taylor, 1999, *Choosing Executives: A Research Report on the Peak Selection Simulation*.)

The Job Candidates

The candidates, three from within the company and one from outside, come from different glass industry careers. One is from marketing, another from manufacturing, a third from finance, and the fourth a scientist whose career has been entirely in research and development. Each enjoys many virtues but is lacking in one respect or another. There are three versions of one candidate: a white female, a black male, and a white male, all with the same career background. According to a rotation scheme made one week prior to the program, this candidate is changed, depending on the racial or gender composition of the team that is performing the simulation.

The four candidates are given exhaustive profiles, including resumes, family background, education, hobbies, news articles, solicited and unsolicited references, and more. Following are brief descriptions of the four candidates.

Candidate A comes to Looking Glass, midcareer, from an air freight business. He is visionary, charismatic, risk taking, persuasive, and creative—very much the "transformational" leader who is all the rage in the current management books written by corporate gurus. We know that he is a maverick and a renegade who derailed in a previous high-level position in another division of Looking Glass (and a little voice tells us that perhaps he also derailed from his previous position, but we don't really have any data to support this). Apparently he learned a lot from that experience and is a much better leader and team player because of it; he no longer makes "end runs" around other executives. We also know that he was an unusual child, reading Faust and Rilke, and that he knew Wagner's Ring cycle by the time he was fourteen.

Candidate B is the quintessential "sleeper" candidate. He is described as quiet, thoughtful, creative, extremely intelligent, and well liked and even loved by his staff. He is a career Looking Glasser, coming up through the engineering ranks with a Ph.D. in chemical engineering and a string of academic publications. Despite this academic background he can speak many corporate "languages," including R&D, manufacturing, and corporate. Although he comes from a background that rewards product and technology myopia, he is quite able to scan a broad horizon and change policies. He "looks" like an executive. He is good-looking, tall, broad-shouldered, and has snow-white hair. He excelled in basketball as a teenager. We even know that his older sister calls him "Teddy Bops," especially in company.

Candidate C is a native of Poland whose family fled to The Netherlands when the Communists took over after World War II. We know "his fondest memories are of his mother's language drills and her Polish beet soup with sour cream." Before he became an executive in the glass industry, Candidate C managed the corporate syndicate department at a London investment banking firm where he specialized in the financing needs of high-technology companies. Later in his career his company invested in specialized fiber optics for photodynamics technology (PDT). We are told that "PDT combines a light-activated compound (a drug), a light source, and a fiber optic delivery system to identify and deactivate abnormal cells and viruses." There is, of course, much more about Candidate C, but not a single "fact" that could not find a real-world analogue.

We learn that Candidate D took no interest in high school athletics but was a good student "who cut a graceful figure on the dance floor." Following military service in Vietnam, he married a beauty queen who was nearly selected as a *Playboy* centerfold. His resume tells us that among his many accomplishments at Looking Glass, he improved "cullet processing through several advanced procedures, including impact crushing, magnetic separation, and air separation; plant scrap loss was reduced from $125,000 per year to $80,000 after one full year."

Participants are given wide discretion in the one-hour computer search. They can ignore self-report information and read only references and descriptions of candidates by others. They can dwell on news articles and unsolicited references, spending little or no time on resumes. They can watch the candidates, each in business dress, answer a variety of questions. The choice is theirs. To read and digest every item in this presentation requires on average two and a half hours, which they are not allowed; as a result, they can look at only a portion of the information that is available to them.

Given the freedom to examine what they wish, each participant comes away with a unique "information profile," which is recorded by the computer program. These profiles represent the "resources" the participants bring into the decision-making meeting.

On the afternoon after the computer-search phase of the simulation, the participants meet in small teams of four to seven members and they are given forty-five minutes to discuss and rank the candidates, top to bottom. These sessions are videotaped. When the discussion ends, the team ranks the four candidates and completes two questionnaires about the team's process and changes in the ranking patterns from their own individual preferences to the team's decision. Debriefings by observers begin immediately. First there is a debriefing of all program participants, which takes about thirty minutes. This debriefing is followed by a two-hour meeting of each small team with the debriefer, during which time the videotape of the team process is shown and the team's performance discussed. A further debriefing of how each participant has done both individually and as a member of the team is included in the comprehensive feedback session on one of the following days for each participant.

Measurement

The Peak Selection Simulation includes measurement at three levels: the individual, the individual within a team, and the team as a whole. There are two main research uses for these data. First, the data reveal how selection decisions are made and the variables that influence the quality of the decision. Second, the data give information about characteristics of leaders and their behavior, at the individual level of analysis. The data are used to examine how individual characteristics of leaders are related to important organizational outcomes.

Bibliography

Barach, J. A., & Eckhardt, D. R. (1996). *Leadership and the job of the executive*. Westport, CT: Quorum Books.

Barnard, C. I. (1950). *The functions of the executive* (8th printing). Cambridge, MA: Harvard University Press. (Originally published in 1938)

Bauer, T. N., Morrison, E. W., & Callister, R. R. (1998). Organizational socialization: A review and directions for future research. *Personnel and Human Resources Management, 16*, 149–214.

Borman, W. C., & Motowildo, S. J. (1993). Expanding the criterion domain to include elements of contextual performance. In N. Schmitt & W. C. Borman (Eds.), *Personnel selection in organizations* (pp. 71–98). San Francisco: Jossey-Bass.

Bournellis, C. (1997, July 14). Amelio resigns after Apple's board sours on him. *Electronic News, 43*, 6–7.

Buckingham, M., & Coffman, C. (1999). *First, break all the rules: What the world's greatest managers do differently*. New York: Simon & Schuster.

Byrne, J. A., Reingold, J., & Melcher, R. A. (1997, August 11). Wanted: A few good CEOs. *BusinessWeek*, pp. 64–70.

Chambers, E. G., Foulon, M., Handfield-Jones, H., Hankin, S. M., & Michaels, E. G. III. (1998). The war for talent. *The McKinsey Quarterly, 3*, 44–57.

Charan, R., & Colvin, G. (1999, June 21). Why CEOs fail. *Fortune*, pp. 69–82.

Ciampa, D., & Watkins, M. (1999). *Right from the start: Taking charge in a new leadership role*. Boston: Harvard Business School Press.

Deal, J. J., Sessa, V. I., & Taylor, J. J. (1999). *Choosing executives: A research report on the Peak Selection Simulation*. Greensboro, NC: Center for Creative Leadership.

Dean, J. W., & Sharfman, M. P. (1996). Does decision process matter? A study of strategic decision-making effectiveness. *Academy of Management Journal, 39*(2), 368–396.

DeVries, D. L. (1993). *Executive selection: A look at what we know and what we need to know*. Greensboro, NC: Center for Creative Leadership.

Drucker, P. (1985, July-August). Getting things done: How people make decisions. *Harvard Business Review*, pp. 22–26.

Exit bad guy. (1998, June 20). *The Economist, 347*, 70–71.

Gabarro, J. J. (1987). *The dynamics of taking charge*. Boston: Harvard Business School Press.

Gabarro, J. J. (1988). Executive leadership and succession: The process of taking charge. In D. C. Hambrick (Ed.), *The executive effect: Concepts and methods for studying top managers* (pp. 237–268). Greenwich, CT: JAI Press.

Gardner, P. D., Kozloski, S. W., & Hults, B. M. (1991, Winter). Will the real pre-screening criteria please stand up? *Journal of Career Planning, 51*, 57–60.

Garrison, S. A. (1989). *Institutional search: A practical guide to executive recruitment in nonprofit organizations*. New York: Praeger.

Grant, L. (1997, May 12). The PepsiCo challenge. *Fortune*, p. 22.

Greco, J. (1997). The search goes on. *Journal of Business Strategy, 18*, 22–25.

Hall, D. T. (1995). Executive careers and learning: Aligning selection, strategy, and development. *Human Resource Planning, 18*, 14–23.

Heller, R. (1997, October). Outsiders' inside track to the top. *Management Today*, p. 21.

Hesselbein, F., Goldsmith, M., & Beckhard, R. (Eds.). (1996). *The organization of the future*. San Francisco: Jossey-Bass.

Hughes, R. L., Ginnett, R. C., & Curphy, G. J. (1999). *Leadership: Enhancing the lessons of experience* (3rd ed.). Homewood, IL: Irwin.

Judge, T. A., & Ferris, G. R. (1992). The elusive criterion of fit in human resources staffing decisions. *Human Resource Planning, 15*, 47–67.

Kaplan, R. E. (1991). *Beyond ambition: How driven managers can lead better and live better*. San Francisco: Jossey-Bass.

Katz, R. L. (1974, September-October). Skills of an effective administrator (with retrospective commentary). *Harvard Business Review*, pp. 90–102. (Originally published in 1955)

Katz, D. R. (1987). *Inside the crisis and revolution at Sears*. New York: Viking.

Katz, D., & Kahn, R. L. (1978). *The social psychology of organizations*. New York: Wiley.

Keller, J. J. (1998, March 27). AT&T handsomely rewarded top brass: CEO Armstrong picked up $1.4 million in salary after year of turmoil. *Wall Street Journal*, p. A3.

Kouzes, J. M., & Posner, B. Z. (1995). *The leadership challenge: How to keep getting extraordinary things done in organizations*. San Francisco: Jossey-Bass.

Kurtzman, J. (Ed.). (1998). *Thought leaders: Insights on the future of business*. San Francisco: Jossey-Bass.

Lawler, E. E. III, & Finegold, D. (1997, November 17). CEO selection: Why boards get it wrong. *Industry Week*, pp. 90–92.

London, M., & Sessa, V. I. (1999). *Selecting international executives: A suggested framework and annotated bibliography*. Greensboro, NC: Center for Creative Leadership.

Mabey, C., & Iles, P. (1991). HRM from the other side of the fence. *Personnel Management*, pp. 50–54.

Mayer, J. D., Caruso, D. R., & Salovey, P. (in press). Emotional intelligence meets traditional standards for intelligence. *Intelligence*.

McCall, M. W. Jr., Lombardo, M. M., & Morrison, A. M. (1988). *The lessons of experience: How successful executives develop on the job*. Lexington, MA: D.C. Heath.

McFarland, L. J., Senn, L. G., & Childress, J. R. (1993). *21st century leadership: Dialogues with 100 top leaders*. Los Angeles: Leadership Press.

Melone, N. P. (1994). Reasoning in the executive suite: The influence of role/experience–based expertise on decision processes of corporate executives. *Organization Science, 5*, 438–455.

Nadler, D. A., & Nadler, M. B. (1998). *Champions of change: How CEOs and their companies are mastering the skills of radical change*. San Francisco: Jossey-Bass.

Nadler, D. A., & Spencer, J. L. (1998). *Executive teams*. San Francisco: Jossey-Bass.

Nicholson, N., & West, M. (1989). Transitions, work, histories, and careers. In M. B. Arthur, D. T. Hall, & B. S. Lawrence (Eds.), *Handbook of career theory* (pp. 181–201). New York: Cambridge University Press.

Noble, B. P. (1995, February 19). The bottom line on 'people' issues. *The New York Times*, p. 23.

Ohlott, P. J. (1998). Job assignments. In C. D. McCauley, R. S. Moxley, & E. Van Velsor (Eds.), *The Center for Creative Leadership handbook of leadership development* (pp. 127–159). San Francisco: Jossey-Bass.

Pfeffer, J., & Viega, J. F. (1999). Putting people first for organizational success. *The Academy of Management Executive, 13*(2), 37–48.

Phillips, J. M. (1998). Effects of realistic job previews on multiple organization outcomes: A meta-analysis. *Academy of Management Journal, 41*, 673–690.

Ryan, A. M., & Sackett, P. R. (1987). A survey of individual assessment practice by I/O psychologists. *Personnel Psychology, 40*, 455–488.

Rynes, S. L., Orlitzky, M. O., & Bretz, R. D., Jr. (1997). Experienced hiring versus college recruiting: Practices and emerging trends. *Personnel Psychology, 50*, 309–340.

Schneider, B., Goldstein, H. W., & Smith, D. B. (1995). The ASA framework: An update. *Personnel Psychology, 48*, 747–774.

Sessa, V. I. (in progress). Executive selection and promotion. To appear in M. London (Ed.), *How people evaluate others in organizations: Cognitive processes in personnel decisions, performance appraisals, and informal judgments*.

Sessa, V. I., & Campbell, R. J. (1997). *Selection at the top: An annotated bibliography*. Greensboro, NC: Center for Creative Leadership.

Sessa, V. I., Kaiser, R., Taylor, J. K., & Campbell, R. J. (1998). *Executive selection:*

A *research report on what works and what doesn't*. Greensboro, NC: Center for Creative Leadership.

Sorcher, M. (1985). *Predicting executive success*. New York: Wiley.

Srivastva, S., & Cooperrider, D. J. (Eds.). (1998). *Organizational wisdom and executive courage*. San Francisco: New Lexington Press.

Top gunning: Qualified CEOs are hard to find. (1997, September). *Managing Office Technology*, p. 33.

Ulrich, D., & Lake, D. (1990). *Organizational capability: Competing from the inside out*. New York: Wiley.

Williams, K. Y., & O'Reilly, C. A. (1998). Demography and diversity in organizations: A review of 40 years of research. *Research in organizational behavior: An annual series of analytical essays and critical review* (Vol. 20, pp. 77–140). Greenwich, CT: JAI Press.

Winkler, K., & Janger, I. (1998, July-August). You're hired! Now how do we keep you? *Across the Board*, pp. 12–23.

Index

tions for, 128–130; team buy-in and, 35–36, 39; team process and, 34–35, 39, 40–41; team-based, 42; trade-offs in, 12, 61–62; types of, 33; used by typical executives, 4–5, 31–32. *See also* Matching process; Team-based selection process

Dell Computer, 16, 61

Delphi Automotives, 83

Development. *See* Employee development; Executive development; Leadership development

Developmental perspective, 9; combining, with selection paradigm, 118, 121, 131; internal candidate hires viewed from, 30, 109–110, 116, 117, 121. *See also* Executive development; Succession planning

Distributed leadership, 137

Diversity: advertising for, 71; in candidate pool, 28, 73–74, 76; fit and, 57, 59; in selection team, 36–38

Downsizing, 5, 133

Drucker, P., 4

Dunlap, A. "C.", 21

E

Eastman Kodak, 16

Emotional component of decision making, 8–9, 88–89, 130

Emotional intelligence, 23, 100

Emotions of applicants, 68

Employee development, as position requirement, 53, 54; internal versus external candidates and, 111

Empowerment skills, 83

Enrico, R., 4–5

Environmental factors: in difficulty of executive selection, 5–6, 133; in organizational results, 25, 26

Ethics, maintaining, as position requirement, 53, 54

Evaluation criteria, 19–25; categories of, 20–25; performance, 21–22, 26; relationship, 22–25, 26

Evaluation of new-hire executives, 104; internal versus external, 97, 116–117; time frame of, 96–97

Executive development, 9, 13, 93–106; continued, as second phase of integration, 99–100, 106, 131; continuing, as

indicator of success, 20; of internal versus external hires, 116; organizational learning system and, 135; percentage of new hires who receive, 94; selection and, 94–95

Executive search firms, 27, 71–73

Executive selection: current state of, 1–17; development and, 94–95, 134, 135; environmental changes and, 5–6, 133; evaluation of success and, 19–30; executive decision makers and, 3–5; executive inattention to, 1–3; executive success and, 19–30; importance of, 1; importance of performance measurement in, 14, 26; of internal versus external candidates, 107–121, 131–132; leadership and, changing views of, 136–139; in organizational context, 133–139; organizational systems and, 134–136; perspectives on, 7–9; reasons for precarious state of, 3–6. *See also* Team-based selection process

Executive Selection: A Research Report on What Works and What Doesn't (Sessa, et al.), 16

Executive success. *See* Success, executive

Executives as selectors, 31–32; decision-making processes used by, 4–5, 31–32, 85–91; lack of selection expertise in, 3, 88–89; minimal self-doubt of, 80, 88; and as networkers, 70–71; personality characteristics of, 3–4, 80; power differential of, 38–39, 43; reasons for inattention of, 3–6; success indicators used by, 19–25; using diverse, 37–38. *See also* Selection team; Selectors

Executives, new-hire. *See* New-hire executives

Expectations: for candidate requirements, 56–57, 62; clarity of superior's, 100; for internal versus external candidates, 30, 121; providing realistic, 67, 68, 74, 76, 101–102, 126

Experience: as candidate requirement, 59, 60, 112; selectors', intuition and, 86–87, 90, 129–130

Expertise, intuition and, 86–87, 90, 129–130

External candidates and hires: in candidate pool, 29–30, 73–74; candidate requirements for, 59–60, 111–113; as

More Titles from the <u>Center for Creative Leadership</u>

Leadership in Action
Martin Wilcox, Editor

Keep yourself up to date on the latest research, findings, strategies, and practices impacting leadership today. *Leadership in Action* offers readers the latest insights from CCL's many ongoing research projects and expert advice on how its findings can best be applied in the real world. Published bimonthly, each issue of this cutting-edge journal delivers in-depth articles designed to help practicing leaders hone their existing skills and identify and develop new ones.

One year (six issues) individual rate: $99.00
One year (six issues) institutional rate: $125.00
Two year individual rate: $158.00 (save 20%)
Two year institutional rate: $200 (save 20%)

Maximizing the Value of 360-Degree Feedback
A Process for Successful Individual and Organizational Development
Walter Tornow, Manuel London, & CCL Associates, Center for Creative Leadership

In this unprecedented volume, CCL draws upon twenty-eight years of leading research and professional experience to deliver the most thorough, practical and accessible guide to 360-degree feedback ever. Readers will discover precisely how they can use 360-degree feedback as a tool for achieving a variety of objectives such as communicating performance expectations, setting developmental goals, establishing a learning culture, and tracking the effects of organizational change. Detailed guidelines show how 360-degree feedback can be designed to maximize employee involvement, self-determination, and commitment. Filled with case examples and a full complement of instructive instruments.

Hardcover   408 pages   Item #F093 $42.95

"This wonderfully useful guide to leadership development will prove an invaluable resource to anyone interested in growing the talent of their organizations."—Jay A. Conger, professor, USC, and author of *Learning to Lead*

The Center for Creative Leadership
Handbook of Leadership Development
Cynthia D. McCauley, Russ S. Moxley,
Ellen Van Velsor, Editors

In one comprehensive volume, the Center for Creative Leadership distills its philosophy, findings, and methodologies into a practical resource that sets a new standard in the field. Filled with proven techniques and detailed instructions for designing and enabling the most effective leadership development programs possible—including six developed by CCL itself—this is the ultimate professional guide from the most prestigious organization in the field.

Hardcover   480 pages   Item #F116 $65.00

"At last, a practical, quick, direct, and easy-to-use tool that helps individuals flex their learning muscles! I'll use the Learning Tactics Inventory (LTI) in my consulting practice right away."
—Beverly Kaye, author, *Up Is Not the Only Way*

Learning Tactics Inventory
Facilitator's Guide & Participant's Workbook
Maxine Dalton

Developed by CCL, the Learning Tactics Inventory (LTI) gives you everything you need to conduct a two- to four-hour workshop that dramatically enhances participants' ability to learn by showing each individual how he or she learns best and how each can adopt new learning strategies accordingly. The *Inventory* is used by workshop participants to profile individual learning styles. The *Participant's Workbook* is used to score and interpret results. *The Facilitator's Guide*, which includes a sample copy of the Participant's Workbook, details all key workshop procedures—including setup, administration, and follow-up—and comes with reproducible overhead and handout masters. You'll need one Inventory and Workbook per participant, available at bulk discounts.

LTI Inventory   paperback   48 pages   Item #G515 $12.95
LTI Facilitator's Guide [includes sample Workbook]   paperback   48 pages   Item #G514 $24.95

Job Challenge Profile
Learning from Work Exerience
Marian N. Ruderman, Cynthia D. McCauley,
Patricia J. Ohlott

Increase career satisfaction and job performance among your
employees with these field-tested tools that help them seek new
challenges and develop valuable new skills in the course of their
professional lives. The *Inventory* will help them profile what and
how much they're learning, where their key challenges lie, and how they can maximize learning in their day-to-day experiences. The *Participant's Workbook* is used to score and interpret
results. The *Facilitator's Guide*, which includes a sample copy of the Participant's Workbook,
contains complete instructions for conducting two- to four-hour workshops. The result will
be the creation of a learning work environment where challenge is welcome and job fulfill-
ment runs high.

JCP Instrument   6 pages   Item #G108 $4.95
JCP Participant's Workbook   paperback   48 pages   Item #G106 $12.95
JCP Facilitator's Guide [includes sample Workbook]   paperback
48 pages   Item #G107 $24.95

Positive Turbulence
Developing Climates for Creativity,
Innovation, and Renewal
Stanley S. Gryskiewicz

Can your company manage—even encourage—turbulence in ways
that actually strengthen its competitive stance? Absolutely. In this
work, top organizational psychologist Stanley Gryskiewicz argues
that challenges to the status quo can be catalysts for creativity, innovation, and renewal and shows leaders how they can keep their company on the competitive edge by embracing a process he calls Positive Turbulence.
Developed through the author's work with many of the world's leading companies over the
course of thirty years, *Positive Turbulence* delivers proven methods for creating an organization that continuously renews itself through the committed pursuit of new ideas, products,
and processes.

Hardcover   2224 pages   Item #E952 $32.95

Leadership and Spirit
Breathing New Vitality and Energy into Individuals and Organizations
Russ S. Moxley

Learn how you can harness your inner spirit to help yourself and those around you approach work with a renewed sense of purpose and satisfaction. In this book, Moxley shows how spirit can spawn a more vital and vibrant kind of leadership—one that, in turn, promotes the creativity, vitality, and well-being of others. Here, Moxley examines various leadership practices: those that elevate people's spirits and those that cause the spirit to wither and wane. He offers specific suggestions on what each of us can do to reach a new level of awareness regarding leadership. And he demonstrates how a spirited leadership that values rituals, celebrations, and employee input creates a totally engaged workforce; one that brings the whole person—mental, emotional, physical, *and* spiritual—to work.

Hardcover 256 pages ISBN 0-7879-0949-1 Item #F115-3C9 $30.95

Available in Bookstores
or Call Toll Free 1-800-956-7739
or Visit Our Web Site at www.jbp.com

Jossey-Bass Publishers
350 Sansome Street
San Francisco, CA 94104